Planet as Self

Planet as Self
An Earthen Spirituality

Sky McCain

Earth Books is an imprint of John Hunt Publishing Ltd., Laurel House, Station Approach,
Alresford, Hants, SO24 9JH, UK
office1@o-books.net
www.o-books.com

For distributor details and how to order please visit the 'Ordering' section on our website.

Text copyright: Sky McCain First Published 2011

ISBN: 978-1-84694-725-4

Design: David Kerby

Printed in the UK by CPI Antony Rowe
Printed in the USA by Offset Paperback Mfrs, Inc

Endorsements

"This is a profound book. The author presents the big picture and shows how humanity can live in harmony with the living earth".

Satish Kumar, Editor, Resurgence

Nurtured by rich personal experiences of nature and much critical reading, the author develops deeply challenging reflections about our attitude to planet Earth and the web of life. He shows how our cultural worldview requires a radical paradigm shift - a new awakening and awareness that moves from an egocentric to an ecocentric consciousness and life stance.

An incisive and most helpful guide for developing an Earth-centred spirituality that is integral and holistic, collaborative rather than competitive, enabling us to become partners and co-creators of Gaia. May this inspiring book find many readers, especially among the young.

Ursula King
Professor Emerita of Theology and Religious Studies
University of Bristol
January 2011

In the tradition of Thomas Berry and Matthew Fox, Sky McCain's book Earthen Spirituality is taking us by the shoulders, giving us a rough shake, and shouting in our faces, "The redemption of humankind lies not with right relationship with some father god in the sky, but in right relationship with our mother the Earth." His book is an articulate and moving cry for a new and global religious reformation, a call to return to sanity that touches not only our bodies and minds, but our spirits as well.

John R. Mabry, former editor CREATION SPIRITUALITY magazine

This book is beautifully written, elegantly argued, heart-*warming* as well as mind-warning and utterly necessary. As a Christian Priest who is also a 'bardic' member of the Order of Bards, Ovates and Druids, I was especially interested in the chapter *Paganism and Christianity*. Here, in relatively few words, the author leaves no stone unturned. He then take us on an exciting journey through the many twists and turns of nature based spirituality, various strands of monotheism and the whole new world of modern science all in relation to the planet that is our home. It is a book that is both theoretical and practical and will enlighten, shock, remind, disturb but most of all re-ignite (or perhaps set on fire for the first time) a deep and passionate love and appreciation for our mother – Gaia – the earth beneath our feet.

Mark Townsend (author of *The Path of the Blue Raven* – O Books)

Contents

To Gaia

Preface

A Further Step in Gaian Perception
"To preserve the natural world as the primary revelation of the divine must be the basic concern of religion."
Thomas Berry

When I first took up the serious study of environmental ethics it was in the hope that I would one day be instrumental in developing a truly Earth-centered ethic. However, the further I got into it, the more I realized that there were already in existence profound ethical statements completely appropriate for living lightly and in harmony with Nature. What my studies and thinking led me to was the opinion that it is not a code of ethics *per se* that we lack but the sort of awareness that would prompt us to put such an Earth-centered code into practice. But how to achieve that?

Scores of inspired thinkers and writers have pointed out that our economics, science and cultural beliefs need to become ecocentric instead of ego-centric. Many of them not only stress the beauty and awesomeness of Nature but rightfully point out how our failure to work with Nature and our attempt to dominate it is causing increasing suffering, destruction and death to a great many of our fellow earthlings of all shapes and sizes. Although I am fully in accord with these observations, the chorus of concerned and passionate voices has so far been ineffective. Why? I suggest that they just don't go far enough. My suggestion is that nothing short of seeing our planet, Gaia, as a living, loving and lovable being will capture people's hearts and move them towards changing their behavior. We and all planetary life are the sensory inputs and outputs of a planetary consciousness. Gaia is not 'out there'. We and all Earthlings *are* the planet. Once we fully recognize ourselves as securely embodied in the fabric of this great being–planet Earth–our hearts and minds will shift into a loving relationship with the true 'ground of our being'.

Acknowledgements

Thanks first and foremost to Marian, my partner and soul mate who has given me the gift of unconditional love and taught me what love really means.

Thanks to Elizabeth Stratton for opening my heart chakra at Esalen Institute those many years ago.

Thanks to the late Jean Klein who gave me what I can only describe as Grace. Through his eyes I saw the utter vastness of 'no-thing ness' and 'every-thing ness'–an infinity of beingness beyond the thinking function and thus beyond description.

Thanks to John Hunt, Chris Clarke and the team at O Books.

Thanks to June Raymond who has helped me to partially overcome some of my limiting beliefs about the role of religion in Western culture.

Thanks also to Seth who does exist.

Thanks to Jesse Wolf Hardin, Loba and Kiva Rose at the Anima Lifeways & Herbal School in the Gila Mountains of southern New Mexico. Jesse now talks and writes about New Nature Spirituality which, however, is no less earthen. It was due to him that I came to revere the term 'Earthen Spirituality'.

The thanking has no end as it coalesces into a benediction of thankfulness itself. Trying to recall and single out teachers along the way reminds me that every person, place or thing I have ever experienced has been a teacher. The search for the right path ends in knowing that there is no path, nowhere to go and nobody going anywhere. There is just the present moment; limitless, unconnected and inconsequential. Being wholly in this moment one is immersed in joy; joy without beginning or end, indescribable and yet known as nothing other than joy. This is a joy in and of being; just being, not being something or somebody or being for. At that no place, there is only the seeing, the hearing, the feeling, the touching, the taste and the deep satisfaction of knowing that we are home.

Sky McCain
www.Earthenspirituality.com
December 2010

3

.

Introduction: An Earthen Spirituality

"The World is the Mirror of your attitude towards it"
Vadim Zeland

Many of us are great seekers of certainty. We press our spiritual and religious leaders for universal truth, always yearning for the definitive answer. Yet all around us we find ourselves immersed in a world where change seems to be everlasting and the only real constant. Unsatisfied and frustrated, we thrust this way and that for answers to life's mysteries as if not knowing was a huge problem. For all who seek, there will always be a few ready answers and there has never been a shortage of spiritual guides. The history of human culture reveals volumes of parchments, scrolls, carvings and cave wall drawings which, taken together, indicate a continuum of change. Over the past five thousand years people have worshipped an endless variety of animals and spirits, all of them projections of cultural ideals. In the last two thousand years, Middle Eastern culture has produced two major sky gods whose followers have engaged in nearly constant warfare with each other over land, property, dogma and religious allegiance.

In the West, our cultural foundations are built around incidents and myths that solidified for over two and perhaps even five thousand years. But now, the dragons appear to have died out and the Earth has become round instead of flat. Today every human may go to heaven instead of only the pharaohs, kings and queens (though the admissibility of other animals remains in doubt). These days, many priests who offer the sacramental wine of Holy Communion admit that it is a symbolic representation of the blood of Christ rather than a literal transubstantiation. A few hundred years ago the church reluctantly relinquished its stranglehold on scientific truth and educated people could then be taught, rightfully, that our planet was not the center of the universe. The firmament (that solid, 'inverted bowl' in which the stars were once thought to be fixed) could not be seen above and the exact location of heaven was acknowledged to be unknown.

Unfortunately, the battle lines between church and spirit on the one hand and science and mind on the other were drawn rather too permanently by Descartes et al who left spirit to the church and glorified the function of human thought. Identifying firmly with that thinking function, they simplified science by just leaving out spiritual matters, hoping perhaps that ruling out spirit would greatly reduce arguments and simplify the game. Descartes' followers developed rites of logical analysis and a scientific method that effectively ignored spirit as if it had ceased to exist. Besides, spirit did not respond appropriately to the approved measuring instruments of the time–and still doesn't. How much love can a liter jug hold? Actually, a being without spirit is as incomprehensible as a computer without main memory. Killing a living being in order to learn about how it 'works' should have been suspect from the very beginning. But alas, there we are.

What Drives My Concern?

The motivation and deep personal concern that informs this writing is coupled with perplexity and disappointment. Yes, I grieve like many for the beings of a thousand shapes who perish during this season of ecocide. I worry about tipping points as I continue to learn and better understand Gaia's behavior. I am uneasy and even fearful as to how Gaia will cope with the loss of the millions of trees and millions of hectares of grasslands that have always played such a vital role in managing the fluctuations in her climate. My question is why, when we know what must be done, do we deflect and argue and doubt and contend?

My disappointment is that seemingly we just don't care enough about Gaia to band together and force our industrial giants to change their cancerous form of capitalism. Is it that we really do care but are in hock to the company store? Are we afraid we shall lose our jobs if we speak out too loudly? Perhaps, but I think the block is hooked into a lower level of subconscious where culturally derived belief systems lie deeply rooted in our psyche.

This book is born out of a desire to answer a question at the end of a chain of thoughts. In the beginning there is the question 'why?'. Why do people participate in the rampant ecocide all around them? Of course, there is the inherently self-destructive foundation of capitalism, an economic cancer demanding growth or death. There is greed and the 'never enough' desire to have more and more. Taking the question to a deeper level, however, reveals to me a lack of love for the planet. Why don't people love the Earth? After years of pondering this question, I came to the conclusion that it is simply because people have not been taught that Gaia is lovable.

A Lovable Planet
If we loved the Earth, we wouldn't act as we do and, moreover, we wouldn't sit back and allow our corporate entities to destroy the health of our environment for the sake of profit. Would we not actively protect our parents and grandparents, our children and friends? Why not earthworms, bees, birds, the air we breathe, and the water we drink?

Continuing along a chain of questions: why have we not been taught that Gaia is lovable? Isn't it simply because we have been taught that we live upon this machine-like mass of solidified molten lava? Most of us and our children today are still taught the mechanistic paradigm that states:

- the Earth is a mechanical structure obeying the laws of Nature known through physics, chemistry and biology
- the Earth is a structure, a thing without consciousness or intelligence; a blob of wheeling bits of matter stuck together by gravity and governed by laws, both known and yet to be discovered
- armed with knowledge of these universal laws all shall

come under our control and Nature will conform to human desires

Moreover, we have also been taught that, contrary to our genetic structural makeup, we are specially deposited here somewhat miraculously by the Creator. Thus with great authority, we have reserved intelligence, soul, spirit, and legal rights strictly for humans.

In the chapters to follow, I will suggest an alternative viewpoint, a viewpoint that is informed by a cooperative venture with Gaia Theory and spirituality. A lot of writing about eco-spirituality and especially 'green' issues comes under the heading of what I call 'you really oughta wanna'. These books tell us where we went wrong and how we should think. I have tried to resist falling into that rut. As I am sure you are aware, hardly a day goes by that someone doesn't publish another article or book illuminating another facet of the breakdown of our culture and the destruction of our environment. Most of these are thick with problems but thin indeed with solutions. Most of the solutions are about what the government or somebody else ought to do.

Our Cultural Worldview is Outdated
Most of us are accepting enough to live in harmony with people of varying beliefs. We see humans as free to believe what they want as long as they don't impinge on others or cause harm. But I suggest that our cultural worldview is deeply destructive, physically, culturally, and psychically. Nobody wants to drink polluted water, breathe polluted air or ingest poisons in our food, so how do we justify our apparent apathy towards the environmental degradation that faces us daily? Why do we seem to just accept the situation as inevitable? Because we hold limiting and sometimes destructive basic beliefs. In this book I call for an examination and re-evaluation of some of these basic beliefs and suggest that they are based on questionable information and lead not only to alienation from our

roots in Nature but ultimately to the destruction of our species and a great many other species around us. Once these toxic beliefs are exposed and examined, I set out in historical perspective how our Western culture's worldview has changed over the last 2000 years. It is important to know that a belief in a living, en-spirited Earth is not a new idea. Nature was at one time seen as a loving and nurturing en-spirited being to be respected and adored. In fact, going back 6,000 years the latest paleontological findings reveal the remains of an advanced culture based on a Goddess religion where the Earth was filled with spirit, life and love. Riane Eisler writes beautifully in her book, *The Chalice and the Blade*, about recent discoveries that can be pieced together to give us some insight into how those ancient people in the Middle East and Western Europe lived. She points out that their social foundation was one of the partnership of male and female; of a socially equalitarian character rather than one of male domination. However, in succeeding years a wave of Aryan invasions brought a radically different way of life which almost completely replaced this much more peaceful culture. The new paradigm, which Eisler calls the 'dominator' model, brought in the following cultural aspects:

- Male dominance and the oppression of women
- Male violence: killing, plunder and slavery
- Generally hierarchic and authoritarian social structure
- Acquisition of wealth by destruction

Of course, their Gods were male.

Steve Taylor, who has also done detailed research on Neolithic cultural beliefs, has the following to say in his book *The Fall*.

I suggested that our modern-day environmental problems stem from our domineering attitude to nature, our assumption that the earth was put there for our own use and so we are entitled to abuse it and exploit it. More precisely, though, I

believe that this attitude itself can be traced back to a more fundamental problem, which is our lack of a sense of aliveness of natural phenomena. To most of us, natural phenomena like trees, rocks, mountains and streams are inanimate objects; we don't see them as beings, with a soul or inner life of their own. However, primal peoples have a completely different relationship to nature. To them all natural things *are* alive, with their own kind of consciousness or inner life.
(Taylor, 2005, p. 95)

Taylor speaks to the heart of the situation that I address in the following chapters. "Primal peoples therefore respect nature because they see it as the manifestation of spirit. And since they see themselves as manifestations of spirit too, they feel a sense of kinship and connection with nature, a sense of sharing identity with it, which contrasts with the sense of 'otherness' to the natural world which we normally experience." (Ibid, p. 96)

Science and Spirituality are Compatible

Can recent scientific research and advancements help with the formulation of an Earth-based spirituality? My answer is yes and I shall give some examples of why I think so.

So along with basic beliefs, we shall be taking a closer look at just what spirituality is and identifying the features of Earth-based spirituality.

Might it be possible, for example, that those spiritual aspects of our lives which the Abrahamic religions teach us to connect with some distant god in some distant heaven are actually spiritual aspects of the Earth itself? Could our felt sense of soul in fact be our tuning in to the soul qualities of Gaia, and are the guardian angels our dim perception of the Earth's unconditional and loving containment of all its creatures?

In the final chapter of the book I shall explain how a new worldview founded on the principle of a living and loving Earth is as valid as the one we have now. Hopefully, I can suggest alternative stories that have as much sense and meaning as those we have been taught, stories that we can honor as our own, rather than tales of ancient ancestors who killed witches and warded off vampires with the sign of the cross. I am encouraged by the following words written by the late Karl Popper, one of the greatest philosophers of science of the twentieth century. "… bold ideas, unjustified anticipations and speculative thought are our only means for interpreting Nature: our only *organon*, our only instrument for grasping her." (1980, p. 280)

My aim is to assist the reader to reach the full potential of a life of radical aliveness and, having shed unworkable basic beliefs, to feel the intense joy from a deep feeling of connectedness and sacred awareness of our Mother Earth. Let me make it quite clear, at the outset, this is not a book about God. This is a book about spirit, specifically the spirit of Gaia. My claim is that Gaia mediates creative energy into a form that we can know, are at one with, and can love. It is an Earthen Spirituality. Why an Earthen Spirituality? Because, as earthlings, we just don't have receptors to commune with the creator of stars and galaxies. Cosmic consciousness leaves some of us cold and unconnected, but sometimes, in quiet precious moments, when totally awash with the wondrous life and beauty around me and overflowing with awe and reverence, I can feel myself immersed in a mutual sharing of the love of Gaia.

A Look at the Konigsee

The dark clouds hang low over the town of Berchtesgarten, Bavaria as I look out of the windows of the B&B I managed to find after my late evening train journey from Munich. After breakfast, I plan to walk to a nearby lake called the Königsee (König's Sea or King Lake). Soon, I am armed with a map and heading south along a road rimmed with forest and farms. There are a couple farmers in their traditional *leiderhosen* feeding cattle still penned up in large barns. The clouds are still hanging low as I walk along the quiet road, glancing left and right.

Suddenly I stop. And I stare in wonderment at the sight that has just appeared in the distance, ahead of me and slightly to the right. The clouds have thinned a little and there, in stark grandeur, is a mountain peak partially covered in snow and ice. The next moment, it is gone. Still trying to catch my breath I find myself eagerly scanning the horizon. Soon, another opening appears and yet another mountain of staggering beauty looks out at me. Of course, I know that I am near the Alps, but up until now I have seen nothing of them. More frequently now, as I walk unsteadily down the road, the clouds grow even thinner and reveal more and more of the mountains around me on both sides. The shocking pleasure is almost more than I can bear as the peaks and ridges steadily emerge from the clouds and the blue sky gradually replaces the grey and white. I'm in a trance now as I approach the lake. Soon I can see that the shores of the Konigsee on both sides dip steeply into the water. At the end of the road is a small level area. I see a tourist boat about to dock. I purchase a ticket to ride, delighted to find that I can just get off anywhere it stops and wander around until the next boat comes by. So at the second stop I get off and walk around a place where thousands of stones from ancient scree have been washed smooth by a mountain stream. I stand in silent aloneness, immersed in the magic of air and water, stone and sky. Oh, to have a loved one here right now: someone with whom to share the beauty of this moment.

1
Gaia and Consciousness

"One regret, dear world, that I am determined not to have when I am lying on my deathbed is that I did not kiss you enough."
Hafiz

The Modern Meaning of the Word 'Gaia'

Throughout the book I refer to our planet Earth as Gaia. Although Gaia was the name of the Earth (more an archetypal power than a Goddess) in Greek creation myth, in the present context it was reintroduced as the name for the living, self-regulating Earth in the Gaia hypothesis formulated in the late 1960s and published in a couple of scientific journals in the early 70s by British scientist James Lovelock. Lovelock, along with microbiologist Lynn Margulis, popularized the hypothesis–which now has the status of a fully-fledged, scientific theory–in a book published in 1979. In an attempt to stay within strictly scientific terminology, they claimed that our planet maintains a stable equilibrium in surface temperature, atmospheric composition, and ocean salinity by means of plant and animal life and acts *as if* it is a living organism in its own right. Many students of Gaia theory, like me, do not feel that life can be fully explained within the strictures of the scientific method, and find overwhelming evidence in Gaia theory to support the belief that Gaia is indeed a living organism, and one of immense power and intelligence.

Our Oneness with the Planet is both Physical and Psychic

Not only are we physically not just **on** the Earth but we are actually **in and of** the Earth, inseparable, somewhat like the relationship of tree leaves to the whole tree. Is a tree the leaves? Is a tree the roots? This oneness is not only physical, but extends to what we falsely separate out as the psychic aspect of our beingness or what some call our consciousness and others our mind. By consciousness I mean more than just self-awareness. I mean the kind of awareness that enables us to witness the thinking, feeling and sensate functions of the body. I like to call our logical, deductive reasoning ability our thinking function and separate it out from the intuitive abilities of our minds. Consciousness can somehow discern the interplay of both of these and give us a sense of being aware at a somewhat higher level than the mere perception of our surroundings.

Gaia as a living being has one body and one consciousness and all of her elements, living and non-living, express this consciousness and are aware of themselves to the extent of their evolutionary development.

David Abram, in his book *Becoming Animal*, speaks both eloquently and beautifully about how our bodies are fully embedded in and part of the very substance of Gaia. He then takes a further bold step by suggesting that it is senseless to think of ourselves as intelligent beings wholly entangled in a mute and senseless, inanimate object that is outside us and totally devoid of a mind of its own. We cannot be separate from the mind of Gaia because we are it. Our science cannot use its instruments to locate it or experiment with it because it is not a separate object to be known. Abram states:

> There is a profusion of individual bodies; there is the enveloping sphere of the planet; and there is the ongoing, open relation between these. The fluid field of experience that we call 'mind' is simply the place of this open, improvisational relationship—experienced separately by each individual body, experienced all at once by the animate Earth itself.
> **(Abram, 2010, p. 127)**

He ends this beautifully written and deeply meaningful chapter with:

Mind, then, as the steady dreaming of this Eairth(sic), the

unseen depth from whence all beings draw their sustenance. Mind as wind, this whooshing force, the medium that moves between and binds all Earthly beings. This mystery rolling in and out of breathing bodies, invisible: wafting up from the soil and gusting down from the passes in vortices and curling waves that splash against the grasses. A fluid receptacle, clear as crystal, for the inpouring fire of sunlight, the pellucid nighttime lens through which our eyes receive the stars. Sentience was never our private possession. We live immersed in intelligence, enveloped and informed by a creativity we cannot fathom.

(Ibid, p. 129)

Gaia is Both Loving and Lovable

The love of Gaia comes through what some have called relational consciousness or a felt sense of belonging, being with and being nurtured. I'm certain it is this phenomenon that excited the beautiful poetry of the nature poets such as Mary Oliver, William Wordsworth, Gary Snyder, Robinson Jeffers and Richard Shelton to name just a few. For me, there is a reciprocal loving energy flowing whenever my heart is open to it and I am not stuck in my thinking function or emotionally unavailable to the moment because of a preoccupation with some inner problem or stress. We can sense Gaia's love and care through every blade of grass as well as spacious mountains, colorful sunsets, a cool breeze on a hot day. Also, love isn't something I have; it is a steady current of the joy in just being that I immerse myself in. Gaia's love is unconditional, enduring, boundless and held in some kind of energy field that is the creative and sustaining force surging throughout her beingness and, as earthlings, *our* beingness.

What indications do we have that Gaia is loving? Pope John Paul II said in 1987 that God loves us unconditionally. Unconditional love, thought of as the highest level of love, means that someone loves us regardless of our character or actions. Gaia circulates and makes available its life-sustaining air and water through an immense and complex circulatory system and favors no particular species. All receive unconditionally. We speak of Nature's bounty when we observe how the plant kingdom produces such an abundance of seeds and fruit that nurture and enable the diversity of beings that partake. Consider the various ways that our planet positions itself and how these movements nurture life. A slowly revolving sphere distributes the rays of the sun. The Earth's tilt causes the seasons which aid the cycles of growth, rest and rebirth. As the Gaia Theory reveals, various life-forms on the planet work in a cooperative way to aid Gaia, the parent organism, in self-regulation. Despite centuries of philosophical discourse on what has been termed aesthetics, exactly what it is eludes us. The pleasure and sense of grandeur some of us feel from seeing beautiful landscape or hearing beautiful music for instance may be the effect Gaia's love has on us.

To speak of the loving energy of Gaia is not to deny the existence of turbulence or the (to us) fearsome aspects of thunderstorms, earthquakes, wildfires and hurricanes. Nor is it to deny any of the 'tough love' aspects that Nature exhibits in the maintenance of ecosystem balance. In Earthen Spirituality, darkness and light are eternally present in equal measures, just like day and night. The breeze that caresses us today may be the gale that blows the roof off our house tomorrow. Our role is not to judge but to accept, to open to the earthy 'isness' of life in both its dark and light aspects and live the fullness of every moment, knowing that we are – and will always be – part of something greater than ourselves, a living planet.

What It is to be Conscious

Iain McGilchrist, a former consultant psychiatrist and neuroimaging researcher presents a very interesting slant on the subject of consciousness. He says:

Is consciousness a product of the brain? The only certainty here is that anyone who thinks they can answer this question

with certainty has to be wrong. We have only our conceptions of consciousness and of the brain to go on; and the one thing we do know for certain is that everything we know of the brain is a product of consciousness... We do not know if mind depends on matter, because everything we know about matter is itself a mental creation... We are not sure, and could never be sure, if mind, or even body, is a thing at all. Mind has the characteristics of a process more than of a thing; a becoming, a way of being, more than an entity. Every individual mind is a process of interaction with whatever it is that exists apart from ourselves according to its own private history.
(McGilchrist, 2009, p. 20)

As McGilchrist demonstrates, the left hemisphere of the brain tends to look out onto a world of things, 'whatnesses', so to speak. However, whereas a thing, a quantity, a whatness can be reduced to separate constituents, a way of being, a quality, a 'howness' cannot be reduced to another. Much confusion and jaundiced thinking can be avoided by not throwing 'whatness' and 'howness' into the same basket and onto the scales. And human consciousness appears to be more of a howness–a process, a quality of being– than a whatness or object.

We are Also the Consciousness of Gaia

Rather than seeing our consciousness as a discrete quality of our humanness, I prefer to see our humanness as a manifestation of a planetary consciousness that in its turn is probably a manifestation of cosmic consciousness and which is expressed through individuals in the same way that the wind plays through a set of wind chimes. This concept of what is sometimes referred to as 'unity consciousness' has been expressed in many major wisdom traditions. It is often associated with a sense of connectedness to everything and a lack of separation from all around you. Adherents claim that the concept of a separate me looking out on an equally separate you and the world outside is an illusion, a falsehood of perception, a misunderstanding of the nature of who we are. There is only one consciousness and it is one that we share with Gaia. In a sense, we, and all life as we know it, are the nerve cells of the planet. There is no separate me, no separate consciousness looking out onto the world. There is only the bodily function of looking: no one doing the looking. Likewise, there is only the hearing, tasting, feeling and no separate consciousness doing these things, no ownership of the seeing.

Please don't be surprised if what I have just said sounds very strange. It might help if you are reminded that modern medical science just cannot tell us physically where the faculty of consciousness, awareness, or the sense of 'me', resides. It has taken me many, many years to work through my basic beliefs and feel comfortable with this idea that I am not strictly my body. Of course, there are many others who are more adept at explaining non-duality. Texts that help have been written by Jean Klein, Nisargadatta, and among the most recent: Lamas Ngak'chang Rinpoche and Khandro Déchen, Francis Lucille, Tony Parsons and Eckhart Tolle. Unity consciousness cuts through whole levels of philosophical orientation but refers to the ultimate and not to our planet. However, all the other attributes of it still apply. Although one of the world's most ancient injunctions is 'know thyself', it is impossible for us to know ourselves in the usual way we have been taught because the knower and the self are one. We are not objects to be known separate from our essence. We can only observe our behavior, the workings of our bodies and remain fully awake and in the present moment; for there is only the present moment. The past and the future are only concepts.

A Transformed Consciousness
Ancient Vedic thinkers and seers taught that an all pervading pure consciousness exists. Abrahamic religions taught that in the beginning there was the absolute consciousness of God. I suggest that this poses a huge, insurmountable problem for us as earthlings. For how do we appreciate and develop a personal, loving relationship with

a cosmic consciousness that spawns stars, galaxies and everything that is? While I can certainly feel awe and reverence for such an entity, it feels too vast to make any sort of personal connection with. Humans simply don't have the receptors for comprehending such immense beingness. However, with Gaia, it is possible to feel such a connection. We can feel it through our five physical senses plus a largely undeveloped intuitive power tuned from birth to our planet's resonant frequency. We have subconscious ways of knowing that can be trusted in addition to paranormal powers. Parapsychologists–the most famous being J.B. Rhine and his wife Louisa of Duke University–have performed thousands of scientific, laboratory experiments designed to test intuitive behavior called extrasensory perception (ESP) such as telepathy, clairvoyance and precognition or future sight. Mainstream scientists (except possibly in Russia) do not accept the validity of ESP, primarily because it does not fit their approved test instruments and it does not fit into accepted theories based on a mechanistic outlook on our world. ESP is so much easier to visualize from the point of view of Gaia and the connectedness of all the members of our own species and all the other species that are known to us. Who knows what other life-forms inhabit the universe? Feeling any sort of connectedness with creatures we cannot even visualize is, for most of us, much too big a stretch.

The Problem of Describing a Planetary Consciousness

There is a major complication arising around the subject of consciousness, especially that of a planetary being. Firstly, we have not developed a language to describe or transmit our awareness of this being. Brian Swimme puts it thus:

A new form of consciousness is beginning to emerge in a small slice of contemporary *Homo sapiens*. As with the early self-aware primates, we are astounded by the new awareness, and when we go to speak of it, we discover that we have no easy or established or efficient way of transmitting this mode of consciousness.

(Swimme, 1996, p. 6)

Of course, pinpointing just where this awareness comes from might be seen by many as absurd and completely unnecessary. But how do I account for the disconnectedness that allows people to profess to love God on Sunday in church and then walk out the door on Monday morning and desecrate the Earth? And that brings us back to the question of why people don't love the Earth. They don't love the Earth not only because they have been brought up with a mechanistic explanation of Gaia, but because they deny Gaia's conscious abilities as if the planet is dumb and doesn't know what it is doing. We are just not taught that Gaia is intelligent, conscious and lovable.

Gaia Transforms Cosmic Consciousness

What if Gaia has a consciousness that has transformed cosmic consciousness? I propose that Gaia, as a huge living being, makes the wonder, diversity and grandeur of the Creator knowable to us as Earthlings. Through a process of coalescence and synthesis, Gaia receives the creative cosmic consciousness that permeates her beingness and creates in her own earthly fashion. Although the process is beyond our understanding, the miracle of photosynthesis may be an example. Perhaps this is what Brian Swimme is hinting at in the following quote from *The Hidden Heart of the Cosmos:*

In the cosmology of the new millennium the sun's extravagant bestowal of energy (The sun, in each second, transfers four million tons of itself into light.) can be regarded as a spectacular manifestation of an underlying impulse pervading the universe. In the star this impulse reveals itself in the ongoing giveaway of energy. In the human heart it is felt as the urge to devote one's life to the well-being of the larger community.

(Swimme, 1996, p. 42)

And maybe Gregory Bateson was onto something similar when he spoke about the "pattern which connects the orchid to the primrose and the dolphin to the whale and all four to me." (Bateson, 1979, p. 8)

Again, what I am proposing here is that the Creator's inestimable energy is transformed by our dear planet. This hypothesis in no way delimits or contradicts the power of God. I am simply suggesting that those feelings and experiences that we have been proclaiming as having come down directly from the Creator are actually coming through to us through Gaia. My thankfulness for just being alive pours out as a child of Gaia and I recognize my love of the Earth. Actually, to speak of *my* love is inaccurate for, as I said above, it is Gaia's love–a current that permeates and sustains our Earthly existence.

The first commandment to the 'chosen people' of the Hebrew bible was that they should love their God. Fine, but how do you get your heart around that energy that creates galaxies and half of creation that we can't even detect? Why even try? What about opening each day to the beauty of the sky? What about honoring the thankfulness and awe that surges through us in those moments when we open ourselves fully to the 'now' moment, especially when we are out in wild and beautiful places? Just recall, for instance, the majesty of waterfalls and grandeur of a mountain rock face. Most of us have had almost heart-stopping moments when we were touched by the glory of Gaia.

Just pause for a moment and imagine the difference in our behavior if we could see the Creator in every delicate leaf and realize that we are so graciously fine-tuned to the energy of a beautiful planet that has received the blessing, so to speak, of the Creator and is so easy to love and be loved by. The first verse of an old song comes to mind:

"How sweet it is to be loved by you."

When we love Gaia, we are loving the Creator as well because the

Creator is not separate from creation. Only now we can see, hear, touch, feel, taste and intuit the Creator as expressed through Gaia. How wondrous. Millions of people search daily for God 'out there' somewhere and ignore and even desecrate their true spiritual home.

Gaia is Worshipful

Let us review what we know about God. Yes, God the Creator. We might start with just what kind of knowledge we have. Is it knowledge that we got from experience or is it handed down? The God of the Old Testament is a Hebrew God, a God looking out for a chosen people. Stories come down to us out of Hebrew history and depict a God of wrath, a jealous God who smites the enemies of the chosen people.

The God of the New Testament as revealed by what are claimed to be the words of Jesus Christ is a God of love and compassion. What happened? Did the Creator change? Our ancient ancestors, understandably, saw love and blessings in the spring rain that coaxed seed from the ground and the sunshine that ripened the fruit. They also saw wrath and punishment in the hailstones that ripped the fruit from the tree and the locusts that devoured the grain. Small wonder, then, that their gods were moody gods who must be propitiated with gifts and sacrifices. It is only now, at this point in the evolution of our consciousness, that we can understand and practice a spirituality that embraces both light and dark and transcends the dichotomy of good and evil.

As I said earlier, we simply do not have the receptors to tune directly into the unimaginable energy and beingness of the Creator. The only option we have had has been to anthropomorphize the Creator and endow 'her' with our own incredibly limited mental and psychic abilities. But I like to think that we are at last growing beyond that limited vision and are now learning to be comfortable with paradox and to stand in reverence before mysteries that our finite minds are probably incapable of grasping. At the same time, we can express our spirituality through our relationship with Gaia. I am reminded of the poem *Abou Ben Adhem* by Leigh Hunt. In this marvelous poem, Abou tells the angel that since his name does not appear in the book of those who love the Lord, then perhaps it could be added to a book of those who love their fellow man. And the next night the angel finds it at the top of the list. So although 'God out there' seems unapproachable and remote, to love the God within Gaia *is* to love God. It is hard to love the distant stars but not hard at all to love our fellow humans and other creatures, mountains, valleys, trees and continents.

Until recently, my tolerance enabled me to simply ignore the more questionable practices of God worship that seemed absurd to me and to see them as really none of my business. Then I saw more clearly how so many people would recite affirmations about the glory of God in church and then turn a deaf ear later to the ecocide and total disrespect for Gaia, our true spiritual home. We are collectively committing suicide and taking thousands of other life-forms with us. And that I *cannot* tolerate. Am I also guilty? Yes, of course. We are all implicitly guilty of our behavior towards Gaia. As humans, none of us is exempt. The last straw for me was realizing that thousands of fundamentalist Christians actually shout with glee when they read about Gaia's destruction as an indication of what they believe to be the necessary path to the Second Coming (see Chapter 4). Thinking that the Creator would destroy that which developed out of love and actually carry out such a ridiculous anthropocentric storyline makes my stomach churn. They should read John 3:16: "for God so loved the world..."

Who Gets to Say What is and What is not Divine?

Astronaut Edgar Mitchell describes Earthrise from the moon:

> Suddenly from behind the rim of the moon, in long, slow-motion moments of immense majesty, there emerges a sparkling blue and white jewel, a delicate sky-blue sphere

laced with slowly swirling veils of white, rising gradually like a small pearl in a thick sea of black mystery. It takes more than a moment to realize that this is Earth... home.
(King, 2009, p. 173)

Ursula King says that Mitchell called it "a glimpse of divinity." And then she continues with: "Is this claiming too much? Earth and nature are not divine. Yet their wonders can lead us to the sphere of Spirit." (Ibid)

I would like to end this chapter with two questions for you to bear in mind as you read further. Firstly, who gets to say what is divine? Secondly, who is in a position to tell Edgar Mitchell that he did not see God?

2
Paganism and Christianity

"If you take [a copy of] the Christian Bible and put it out in the wind and the rain, soon the paper on which the words are printed will disintegrate and the words will be gone. Our bible IS the wind."

Anonymous Native American woman

The foundation of the present is made from the building blocks of the past. There appears to be a deep-seated yearning within us to seek out and find the 'real' world, i.e. the world as it really is. Many of us, however, have come to the conclusion that we are stuck with our 'filters'. These limit us to a reality based on our individual genetic makeup coupled with our particular environment and our personal life experiences. Thus, although we are all members of the same species and descended from common ancestors, each individual sees a slightly different world.

Bronislaw Szerszynski, in the preface of his book *Nature, Technology and the Sacred*, points out that present relationships, with Nature and technology for instance, "have been shaped by those of the past." Sometimes we swear to an objectivity as if we were somehow able to stand at a point outside of the Earth, looking in and talking about how things are. Szerszynski cites Hans-Georg Gadamer, the father of modern hermeneutics, the theory of interpretation. Gadamer, a German philosopher, taught that people have a "historically affected consciousness" and are embedded in both the past and present of the culture that formed them. This applies especially as regards contact with the natural world. Love and concern for Nature are difficult to teach because Western urban culture and much of the countryside, with its highly mechanized farming sector, has so isolated and alienated itself from Nature that attempts to commune with the natural world are too far outside our cultural context. 'Back to Nature' attempts have not been very successful. Is there really any reachable wilderness left to visit? And even if you did manage to get there, could you stay long enough, alone, to actually feel into and benefit from the experience? Probably not.

Two major cultural movements had a major impact on how we see ourselves in relation to Nature. Both had a profound effect on the religious and spiritual context of people in Western Europe and later in the Americas. They are Christianity and Renaissance science. In this chapter we shall look briefly at how Christianity undermined and nearly destroyed established religious practices and values that taught beliefs in an en-spirited planet.

Let me begin by digging up some of the remains of the history and major beliefs of Pagan mysticism in order to establish that some pre-Christian European tribes worshipped, loved and respected an en-spirited planet. This is a difficult task for several reasons. Firstly, spiritual practices were passed along orally and what might have survived in writing did not survive the enmity of the Romans and Christians who wished to supplant Pagan beliefs with their own. Secondly, what text we can find was often written by Christians, monks perhaps, who were not exactly dedicated to putting a friendly face on the subject. From Ireland, for instance, almost nothing about Celtic beliefs was written down. Thirdly, the Druids, movers and shakers of pagan peoples (see below) explicitly forbade the writing down of their methods and procedures. So when the Druids, in their stronghold in Anglesey, Wales, were largely wiped out by the Romans in 60 AD (see below) much was lost to us and very little remains from other areas and sources.

Pagan Europe
We shall refer to the religion and spiritual beliefs of the late Iron Age Indo-European peoples as Paganism. 'Pagan' is the word for 'country dweller'. After the last ice age when fertile river valleys became available and people discovered that stored grain would grow, the prevailing hunter-gatherer culture gradually transitioned into an agricultural economy and people began to live together

more closely in farming settlements. Spiritual beliefs became more sophisticated, organized and codified. The Grecian and Roman religions were some of the most highly developed. The following discussion concerns Paganism as found in Northern Europe at the time of the Roman invasion of Gaul focusing on just one of the many Pagan peoples, the Celts who inhabited the British Isles when the Romans moved south from the continental area they called Gaul around 50 AD. Although beliefs and practices varied somewhat across Eastern, Central and Western Europe, lumped together they all came to be known as Paganism. Paganism is Earth-based. In Pagan communities, natural objects were thought to be imbued with spirit and some were worshipped as gods and goddesses. Pagans saw the divine in Nature. Heavenly bodies, rivers, trees, mountains and especially large stones were venerated. These deities influenced all of life's activities. Pagans personified the land, sky and sea by associating these areas with individual gods and goddesses. The religion of the Megalithic peoples (nameless peoples known for their burial grounds called dolmens) and Celts can be primarily described as a belief in magic. Those who knew the power of certain natural substances, mineral or vegetable, to produce bodily and mental effects were magicians and thought to embody the 'magical' properties of life. Although they had no concept of a heaven or hell, they did believe in reincarnation. It is more accurate to speak of the Celts as a culture rather than a race of people. Celtic culture had spread across northern Africa, on into Western Europe and over into England by at least 500 BC. Most of what we know about the Celts of Western Europe comes from Roman descriptions. Not even a shortened background description about the Celts would serve without a mention of Druidry.

Although not a lot of information about them has survived, The Druids were the men and women sages, magicians and wise priests of the Celts.

The unifying bond between all the Celtic tribes was their

common priesthood, the Druids. Their efforts preserved common culture, religion, history, laws, scholarship, and science. They had paramount authority over every tribal chief and, since their office was sacred, they could move where they wanted, settling disputes and stopping battles by compelling the rival parties to arbitration. They managed the higher legal system and the courts of appeal, and their colleges in Britain were famous throughout the Continent. Up to twenty years of oral instruction and memorizing was required of a pupil before being admitted into their order. Minstrels and bards were educated by the Druids for similar periods. Knowledge of the Druids comes directly from classical writers of their time. They were compared to the learned priesthoods of antiquity, the Indian Brahmins, the Pythagoreans, and the Chaldean astronomers of Babylon. Caesar wrote that they 'know much about the stars and celestial motions, and about the size of the earth and universe, and about the essential nature of things, and about the powers and authority of the immortal gods; and these things they teach to their pupils.' They also taught the traditional doctrine of the soul's immortality. They must have professed detailed knowledge of the workings of reincarnation, for one writer said that they allowed debts incurred in one lifetime to be repaid in the next. A significant remark of Caesar's was that Druidism originated in Britain, which was its stronghold. Indeed, it has all the appearance of a native religion, being deeply rooted in the primeval native culture. Its myths and heroic legends are related to the ancient holy places of Britain, and they may largely have been adapted from much earlier traditions.
(Michell)

When Druids in Britain repeatedly aided the Pagans in Gaul, the Roman governor Suetonius Paulinus in 60 AD attacked the Druid stronghold on the isle of Mona (Anglesey) and slaughtered the very heart of the Druid resistance plus most of their sacred groves. The Druids never recovered their former religious strength and influence and only re-emerged in the eighteenth century sans the sacred wisdom of their ancestors.

The Status of Women in the Pagan World

Women were held in very low esteem in Roman pagan culture. They were not allowed to vote or engage in politics. Married at puberty, they were expected to produce and educate boys and it would be fair to say were little more than concubines in social status. They were forbidden to drink wine and could be killed by a relative for adultery. They had no choice in marriage and, if divorced, had no rights to depart with their children. Understanding, therefore, how women's lives were circumscribed in those times makes it easier to understand why the writings and influence of women in the early church were largely purged from accepted scripture when Christianity became the new Roman state religion.

The Christian God of War

Turning now to the spread of Christianity and looking back to the period just before the Romans pulled out of Gaul, we find a political environment in which the few Christian converts in Britain suffered persecution. However, In 313 AD, after a surprising Christian conversion following a battle (see below), the Emperor Constantine granted them freedom to worship as they chose. Cut off from the church in Rome, Celtic Christians formed distributed groups centered on monasteries rather than dioceses and developed distinctive practices centered on local leaders and spiritual practices.

When the Romans pulled out of England around 410 AD, they left a power vacuum which was filled from abroad. In the fifth and sixth centuries, Saxons, Angles and Jutes from Germany and Danish warriors invaded southern and eastern England and gradually took over. Christianity was greatly diminished in England, less so in Cornwall.

Western Christianity formally fell under the power of the Roman Empire at the first Council of Nicaea in 325 AD.

> The Christian tradition of God as the warrior began in 312 AD with the Roman Emperor Constantine. After a major victory in battle against legions of his brother-in-law, Constantine said he had prayed for divine help before the engagement and then had a vision of a cross in the sky above his soldiers as they marched into the fray. This mystical event led to his Christian conversion.
> **(Turnipseed, 2005)**

Tom Turnipseed continues to explain how Christianity was corrupted by the Roman Empire:

> It had been unlawful for a Christian to be a soldier in the Roman army, but Constantine's conversion abruptly allied Christianity with Rome's military and by AD 416 it was compulsory for all Roman soldiers to be Christians. Constantine's army carried a cross as a standard that was a spear with a bar across it, exchanging the symbol of Jesus' death as an innocent victim of oppression for a symbolic weapon of the oppressor. The church took up the sword, and Christian participation in many wars and crusades since has been done in the name of God. The nonviolent image of Christ the peacemaker was transformed into the martial God.
> **(Ibid)**

Although Christians were no longer persecuted, the loving and compassionate example set by Jesus Christ not much more than 300 years earlier was largely ignored.

Ramsay MacMullen, the award winning classical Roman scholar, has conducted an exhaustive study of *Christianity and Paganism in the Fourth to Eighth Centuries,* in his book by this title. The following information has been taken from this source. "The Christians, not only in their triumphant exaggerations but in their sheer bulk, today, seriously misrepresent the true proportions of religious history." (MacMullen, 1997, p. 3) Very few non-Christian documents about paganism survived the early days because they were ceremonially burned. Pagan texts had little value for early Christians especially since those who touched them could have their hands cut off as a punishment. Early Christianity actually grafted itself onto the foundation of Paganism throughout the remains of the Roman Empire. Christianity did not out-compete the established religious beliefs but gradually substituted Christian themes, many created fresh from the numerous councils (ecclesiastical meetings) in the place of Pagan ones.

Readers may be interested in the answers to the following two questions. How were people with established religious practices converted? And how did Christianity achieve such immense success in supplanting native religion in so many countries? As regards the first question I suggest that there were two quite successful methods commonly used. Firstly, as was noted above, divine emperors of Rome, starting with Constantine, converted to Christianity, and in the late fourth century made Christianity the state religion. However, from the beginning, the Emperors chose the church leaders who in turn sanctified the belief structure and controlled many political appointments. By the late fifth century, Pagans were banned from all imperial service including lawyers and teachers in schools. "Temples were broken up and sacred trees felled... anyone who resisted was beaten and flogged." (Ibid, p. 68) However, just as persecution of Christians in the first three centuries reinforced Christian zeal and determination, the subsequent persecution of the Pagans by the now victorious Christians failed to completely eliminate Pagan rites and ceremonies. "To the surprise of Constantine Porphyrogenitus in the tenth century, a little corner of southern Greece still sheltered a wholly idolatrous, good-old-fashioned Greek population." (Ibid, p. 66) The very tools that were used on Christians by the Roman government were later used on Pagans by the Christian Church. Neither party achieved their goals. Many Pagans officially converted to keep their jobs, property and social status while privately worshipping as they had done in the past.

Secondly, superstitious beliefs were transferred from Pagan sources to martyrs, saints and monks; especially those who claimed that they could perform miracles or held healing powers. Many converted out of fear caused by the Christian teachings about the wretched underworld and to avoid evil spirits incorporated into the concept of 'the devil'. In parallel with the conversions was the persistence of Pagan rites and rituals. The January Kalends was observed in Constantinople until at least the mid sixth century. The festal calendar was filled with events such as the Roman Brumalia in November, the birthday of Helios and the winter solstice on 25 December, the equinox and March festivals to name just a few (Ibid, p. 39). Even the most well-known religious holidays observed today, such as Easter Sunday and Lent, are Pagan in origin. Easter comes from the worship of Ostara or Eostre the Anglo-Saxon goddess of spring and the 40-day fasting of Lent began with Sumerian fertility goddess Inanna. There are in modern times at least six Catholic patron saints of fertility. For a more qualified insight, I refer the reader to Edward Gibbon, the first modern historian of the Roman Empire. Of the five causes proposed by Gibbon, the following cause seems to me to be the strongest. "The union and discipline of the Christian republic, which gradually formed an independent and increasing state in the heart of the Roman Empire." (Gibbon, 1782) Since the sixteenth century it has been generally known as evangelicalism. Further:

> The promise of divine favor, instead of being partially confined to the posterity of Abraham, was universally proposed to the freeman and the slave, to the Greek and to the barbarian, to the Jew and to the Gentile. Every privilege that could raise the proselyte from Earth to heaven, that

could exalt his devotion, secure his happiness, or even gratify that secret pride which, under the semblance of devotion, insinuates itself into the human heart, was still reserved for the members of the Christian church; but at the same time all mankind was permitted, and even solicited, to accept the glorious distinction, which was not only proffered as a favor, but imposed as an obligation. It became the most sacred duty of a new convert to diffuse among his friends and relations the inestimable blessing which he had received, and to warn them against a refusal that would be severely punished as a criminal disobedience to the will of a benevolent but all-powerful Deity.

(Ibid)

The point that I wish to especially emphasize and have saved for last was devastating for Gaia. One extremely significant practice did not survive. As I have pointed out above, Pagans worshipped the forces of Nature directly. With the advent of Christianity, the worship of saints and martyrs took the place of Nature, especially in the area of healing and the warding off of evil spirits. Thus, looking at healing waters, for example, worshippers no longer appealed directly to Nature but instead invoked the aid of intermediaries such as saints and martyrs who controlled and invoked the power of Nature. Christian converts and subjects were taught that the healing powers of Gaia that were freely available to all under Paganism were only thereafter available through channels sanctioned by the church. The only spirit allowed was the holy spirit, part of a triune god or the holy trinity decreed at the Council of Nicaea in 325 AD and chaired by King Constantine sitting on the throne as the sun God. Over the next thousand years the ecclesiastical power of the Roman Catholic Church grew stronger and more corrupt until the well-known Protestant revolt commonly called the Reformation.

The Far-reaching Effect of the Reformation

Protestantism seriously challenged the church's spiritual authority and power. The church claimed its authority was handed down directly from Saint Peter who held the keys to the kingdom so to speak. Now thousands of people were told that God's authority came from the Bible and, most important, that people could obtain grace directly from God – bypassing the priest. A further departure was the Protestant doctrine that one could be saved by faith alone. The deeper issues here that are pertinent to a cultural worldview are those of power and order, especially when order serves the illusion of certainty. Protestantism created a power and certainty vacuum previously held by the authority of the church. Personal interpretation of the Bible lacked the infallibility claimed by the Pope. The church appeared to be more concerned about obedience than faith. One doesn't necessarily have to be faithful to be obedient. I suggest that church doctrine ill-prepared people to assume responsibility for their own destiny and rendered them unable to deal with the diversity of multiple interpretations of the Bible. This dilution of power and lack of certainty after the Reformation disturbed the order that had been inherent in the church and created a certainty vacuum. As we will see in the next chapter, this certainty vacuum was filled by the growth and development of a mechanistic science that took the life and soul out of a Nature already discarded by the church.

At Cave Creek Canyon

Shade is slowly creeping up the distant canyon wall below as I sit quietly looking out over the tops of the trees. There are no other campers, so I can hear the faint sounds of the canyon as birds, insects and only a few animals prepare for the end of the day. I am too low in elevation for brown bears. Every campsite in the American Southwest has its 'moocher' (its creature who hangs around in the hope of freebies). Soon the Cave Creek moocher shows itself. A skunk. The skunk fearlessly snuffles around my feet, seemingly unconcerned by my human scent. It does the rounds of the campsite, busily searching for some discarded morsel or some hapless insect. There will be no tent over me tonight so I make a note that I must remain quiet and unalarmed by this skunk's inevitable visit. (I think slapping a skunk around at 1:00 a.m. will not be a happy camper activity.) As the light diminishes and clouds darken, I hear, against the *pianissimo* background of the running water, the wind rustling the leaves higher up the canyon and moving my way. A gentle cooling breeze then moves over me from below and rustles through my beard. My heart seems to pause and I feel caressed by an ephemeral lover. It triggers a memory of the strange sound I had heard that afternoon while walking along the creek. It was an odd, unfamiliar noise, a quiet burble in the distance. What is it? I asked myself. Then, astonished, I found myself looking at the water curling over a tiny waterfall and emitting a sound I'd never before encountered. Sixty years of creek exploration and a totally new sound. Have I not been blessed?

Throughout the day, pillows of grey and white clouds have been skipping along over the low mountain peaks, some lingering as if to catch a better view of the canyon. Now, they begin to color with salmon pink, some already showing their grey underbellies. The clouds bring a feeling that seems to connect all the pleasant experiences of my past with this present moment and I am overwhelmed with a kind of grace. As the opposite creek bank slides slowly into darkness, I pick up movement. Ah, yes, the skunk climbing the rocks. There are no other humans for miles around but I am neither alone nor lonely.

3
A Mechanistic Science

"Science can and should take us to a place where we exclaim 'how
wonderful creation is'."
Laura Smith

Many early scientists were philosophers who had a keen interest in
discovering more about the laws of Nature and the inner workings
of both the Earth and the universe. Unfortunately, not only did
the church's power concern itself with spiritual issues but church
doctrine essentially pronounced on philosophy and basic beliefs
about the nature of reality. Both the church's power structure and its
hold over people's beliefs were nearly absolute. Any disagreements
expressed by thoughtful people of whatever rank and privilege
were cruelly repressed, often through excommunication, sometimes
preceded by an inquisition and then many times ending by being
burned at the stake. Giordano Bruno came to such an end.

Nicolaus Copernicus, Giordano Bruno and Galileo Galilei
Copernican heliocentrism is the name given to the theory, developed
by Nicolaus Copernicus, that the Earth revolves around the sun.
This was a total reversal of Ptolemy's geocentric (the sun goes
around the Earth) model that had held sway as truth since 150 AD.
Copernicus founded modern astronomy and first published his
heliocentric theory of planetary movements in 1543. However, the
Copernican system simply did not fit into the Aristotelian way of
thinking. The church's fanatical opposition to heliocentrism was
founded not so much on disagreement with the scientific data but
on the implications. As Anne Primavesi explains, it was the position
of man as "central to God's concerns and as God's representatives
on Earth" (Primavesi, 2003, pp. 4-5) that was the real issue. It
promoted and supported the belief that "we are somehow entitled

to the dominant position here" (on Earth) (Ibid).

Arthur Koestler makes this point very clearly in his book *The Sleepwalkers*. He outlines the basis of medieval thought which was a closed, static system whose details were incorporated in the publications of the ancient Greeks, especially Aristotle. Koestler stresses that it was the implications from the ideas of Copernicus that upset the church. He says: "The Aristotelian universe was centralized. It had one center of gravity, one hard core, to which all movement referred." (Koestler, 1959, p. 220) With the Copernican universe "...the directions 'up and down' are no longer absolute, nor are weight and buoyancy." And "... the reassuring feeling of stability, of rest and order are gone; the Earth itself spins and wobbles and revolves in eight or nine simultaneous different motions." (Ibid, p. 221) Here again, the sense of certainly was at stake and the stakes were exorbitantly high. Fearful for his life, Copernicus wisely dedicated his work to the Pope and kept a very low profile, and his head, by publishing a polished piece only just before he died.

Giordano Bruno, however, was not so fortunate. He was "working with the principle of the association of ideas, and continually questioning the value of traditional knowledge methods." (Kessler) Further, "A new astronomy had been offered to the world at which people were laughing heartily, because it was at variance with the teachings of Aristotle. Bruno was carrying on a spirited propaganda in a fighting mood." (Ibid) Between the years 1582 and 1592 there was no one but Bruno teaching about the universe as conceived by Copernicus. Bruno barely escaped the Inquisition several times. However, after being imprisoned for the previous eight years in Rome, he was burned at the stake for heresy in 1600.

Over 30 years later, one of the most illustrious thinkers of the century, Galileo Galilei (1564-1642 AD), astronomer and physicist, pushed his opposition to the outdated and inaccurate Aristotelian worldview to the limit his popularity would allow.

He was a passionate, powerful character who could dominate

any room or discussion. His talent and wit won a variety of illustrious friends in university, court and church circles. At the same time his biting sarcasm against those whose arguments were vulnerable to his scientific discoveries made him some formidable enemies. Galileo thrived on debate... His professional life was spent not only in observing and calculating but also in arguing and convincing. His goal was to promote as well as develop a new scientific worldview. **(Hummel, 1986, p. 82)**

What followed was the arrogant refusal of the church to accept dissention from church-sanctioned truth. The church's attitude was that if Aristotle was wrong then the bible was wrong and the Holy Scripture just could not be seen as being wrong.

The Holy Tribunal in Galileo's condemnation states: "The proposition that the sun is the center of the world and does not move from its place is absurd and false philosophically and formally heretical, because it is expressly contrary to the Holy Scripture. The proposition that the Earth is not the centre of the world and immovable, but that it moves, and also with a diurnal motion, is equally absurd and false philosophically, and theologically considered, at least erroneous in faith." **(Rohr, 1988, p. 24)**

From the Holy Tribunal's statement cited above, one may get the impression that the church decided the validity of faith, not the individual. So the issue came to be facts or faith and the church controlled the validity of both.

In 1633, Galileo was found guilty of heresy, his book was banned, and he was forced to claim that he had been wrong, that the Earth did not move. He was then placed under house arrest for the rest of his life. It has been reported that after admitting that the Earth did not move, he muttered under his breath, "However, it *does* move."

"To the popular mind, the Galileo affair is prima facie evidence that the free pursuit of truth became possible only after science 'liberated' itself from the theological shackles of the Middle Ages." (Johnston)

Sixteenth and Seventeenth Century Development of Science

To understand more fully the massive effect modern science has had on our relationship with Gaia and with Nature, it is necessary to brush a broad stroke through the sixteenth and seventeenth century development of science. For this I have drawn heavily from the exacting research of Carolyn Merchant in her book, *The Death of Nature*. In sixteenth century Europe: "the root metaphor binding together the self, society, and the cosmos was that of an organism. Vital life permeated the cosmos to the lowliest stone." (Merchant, 1982, p. 1) Vitalist philosophical positions can be traced back to antiquity. There was Aristotle, the Greek Stoics, Galen, and later Paracelsus and Henri Bergson to name a few.

(Vitalism) posits that living things have a spirit or life force which sustains them and/or imbues them with power. However, the pressure of commerce and technological innovation that brought on the commercial and industrial revolution demanded changes, not only in the way society viewed nature, but in the ethics that underpinned how nature was to be exploited to support commercial and technological growth. These two forces successfully undermined the "organic unity of the cosmos and society.
(Ibid, p. 5)

Bear in mind that this change was gradual. Renaissance Nature was depicted as a woman. In pastoral poetry and art, for instance, the woman was depicted as passive and compliant to the needs of commerce and industry. "Both pastoral art and Aristotelian philosophy saw the female sex as passive and receptive." (Ibid, p. 20) The scene was thus set for the passivity of matter to be "incorporated into the new mechanical philosophy in the form of inert, 'dead' atoms, constituents of a new machine-like world in which change came about through external forces, a scheme that readily sanctioned the manipulation of nature." (Ibid) Thus the self-sustaining integrity, the living essence of an organic being was destroyed to be replaced by moving 'bits' which could be replaced by other moving 'bits' which could be controlled by mathematics and mechanical laws. These were now purported to be laws of Nature. An ordered universe controlled and imbued with a spiritual life force was gradually replaced by arrangements of dead matter organized into machines that obeyed the laws of mathematics and physics. As the use of machines grew hand in hand with the growth of capitalism, wealth and the utility of machines demonstrated the new order of Nature, a Nature now 'managed' by scientists and machinery.

Human Exploitation of Nature
One of the most prominent spokespersons for the human exploitation of Nature was Francis Bacon (1561-1626). Bacon devised the inductive method of enquiry to establish the dominion of man over Nature and believed that "Nature must be 'bound into service' and made a 'slave', put 'in constraint' and 'molded' by the mechanical arts." (Merchant, 1982, p. 169)

Thomas Hobbes (1588-1679), one of the founding philosophers of materialism, moved mechanism into the social realm in his work *The Leviathan*. He developed a mechanical model of society. Competition among equals was to be replaced by cooperation mediated by a sovereign. It is interesting to note that the mechanical model of physical Nature put forth by a mechanistic philosophy was applied to society in the same way that physical evolution of plants and animals was applied to society by Herbert Spencer. Taking the results of research from one set of objects and applying them to another with the assumption that they are equally valid is unacceptable logic. The driver for this kind of misplaced logic is usually personal or group gain. Many people fall for it without question. Merchant very clearly points out that:

> The rise of mechanism laid the foundation for a new synthesis of the cosmos, society, and the human being, construed as ordered systems of mechanical parts subject to governance by law and to predictability through deductive reasoning. A new concept of the self as a rational master of the passions housed in a machinelike body began to replace the concept of the self as an integral part of a close-knit harmony of organic parts united to the cosmos and society. Mechanism rendered nature effectively dead, inert, and manipulable from without. As a system of thought, it rapidly gained in plausibility during the second half of the seventeenth century. Its ascendancy to status as a new worldview was achieved through combating some presuppositions of the older organic view of nature while absorbing and transforming others.
>
> **(Ibid, p. 214)**

And further, "Among its greatest strengths were that it served not only as an answer to the problem of social and cosmic order, but it also functioned as a justification for power and dominion over nature." (Ibid, p. 215) Interest in Nature was institutionalized into a managerial approach that defined the worthiness of Nature according to how well it served human ends. Thus a great deal of environmental ethics became pragmatic. Carolyn Merchant beautifully sums up her thesis in these words:

> Both order and power are integral components of the mechanical view of Nature. Both the need for a new social and intellectual order and new values of human and machine power, combined with older intellectual traditions, went into the restructuring of reality around the metaphor of the machine. The new metaphor reintegrated the disparate

elements of the self, society, and the cosmos torn asunder by the Protestant Reformation, the rise of commercial capitalism, and the early discoveries of the new science.

(Ibid, p. 234)

In the following chapter, I shall draw out some possible reasons why I believe that our cultural worldview is deeply destructive: physically, culturally, and psychically. You are invited to examine some of our society's deeply held attitudes, many of which are based on outdated and destructive basic beliefs.

4
The Problem with Basic Beliefs

"To destroy the stereotypes of the usual worldview, in order to break free from the box of conditionality and to wake up in the dream, you are dreaming awake."

Vadim Zeland

"We have a sufficiently strong propensity not only to make divisions in knowledge where there are none in nature, and then to impose the divisions on nature, making the reality thus conformable to the idea, but to go further, and to convert the generalizations made from observation into positive entities, permitting for the future these artificial creations to tyrannize over the understanding."

Henry Maudsley

"Even beyond the threat of nuclear warfare, I think, the ecological crisis is the greatest threat mankind collectively has ever faced… My hypothesis is that man is hampered in his meeting of this environmental crisis by a severe and pervasive apathy which is based largely upon feelings and attitudes of which he is unconscious."

Harold Searles

Knowing the Earth as a living being may require a realistic examination of the basic beliefs that most of us absorbed as children. A solid belief structure that unconsciously assists the ego in keeping balance is an important part of the way our minds work. What I think we need to realize is how many of our basic beliefs are built out of cultural beliefs that were formed by people without access to the knowledge base of modern culture. It is as if all modern music composers were limited to Gregorian chants or writers had to use Olde English. Brian Swimme, in his book *The Hidden Heart of the Cosmos*, describes and provides examples of the immense chasm separating religious approaches to our place in the cosmos and the context of our physical presence within a planet revolving around a sun as part of a galaxy among millions in the universe. He says, "… within our religions, when we do ponder the deep questions of meaning in the universe, we do so in a context fixed in a time when the classical scriptures achieved their written form." (Swimme, 1996, p. 11) Why put new wine into old wineskins?

Learned Perceptions
The use of our prefrontal cortex allows us to be self-conscious and self-reflective. However, we can choose to override our instincts and even ignore them. Our ability to 'learn' perceptions is so advanced that we can actually acquire perceptions indirectly from teachers The trouble is that learned perceptions may be stored as 'truths'. When these truths turn out to be false, they can and often do cause limiting, disrupting and sometimes destructive behavior. According to Bruce Lipton, a cell biologist, beliefs control biology. Lipton's research reveals that our beliefs affect genetic activity. The well-known placebo effect is one example. Thinking that we need to regulate and control a dumb planet is another one of those erroneous beliefs which may cause our ultimate extinction.

What I am advocating in this book is a serious examination of our life experiences, past and present, in the light of what we now know about Gaia, the living planet. I invite my readers to look deeply within themselves for the foundation principles that underpin their opinions and preferences; to open up their book of basic beliefs and examine it in the light of its relevance to life in the present century. Why do I suggest that this is necessary? As I mentioned in the introduction, we humans have been totally unable to limit our numbers and lifestyles to fit the capability of our planet to cope with us. Although nobody would deny that we rely on the soil, water and air around us for our health and well-being, we persist in poisoning ourselves. Our masculine dominated governments settle their differences by fighting to the death. Why? I suggest that we need to answer this question and quickly.

The media are constantly pointing to our ecological crisis with example after example. In November 2009 I read in the BBC News that, according to a poll, fewer than half of Britons believe that human activity is to blame for global warming. In January 2010, an American survey revealed that only 47 percent of Americans think global warming is caused mostly by human activities. This is after repeated measurements and an overwhelming acceptance by the scientific community that although climate change is a natural phenomenon, our activities are contributing hugely to some seriously negative climate changing factors such as the increase of greenhouse gasses in the atmosphere. This is shocking. What I found even more shocking is a report that thousands and thousands of Christian fundamentalists believe the Earth was created around 6,000 years ago. Tolerance is a virtue, but I, for one, can no longer remain silent while the foundation of my life crumbles around my feet and I wonder what Earthly life will be like for my grandchildren and great-grandchildren. Becoming aware of the new scientific data that might give us fresh insights and encourage alternative viewpoints, such as the Gaia Theory, does not seem to result in lifestyle changes. What governs our acceptance of a new idea? Despite our acceptance of both theoretical and experiential data, the data must make its way through the filters of our worldview. The trouble is that our thinking function can readily accept certain facts but their meaning and the relationship with what we already know is often altered by our worldview. Some people call this phenomenon 'failure to connect the dots'.

Quantum physics, systems theory, and Earth sciences shout loudly for a paradigm shift of our basic beliefs as to the nature of reality. Whether these recent findings have raised our collective consciousness or deepened our collective awareness seems debatable. However, it is all too obvious that we need to re-evaluate our story. Suggestions concerning how our new science can be used to bolster our beliefs will be elaborated on in Chapter 6. Right now, let's examine some of the limiting basic beliefs that prevail in our culture.

Anthropocentric View of Creation in Genesis

A very important limiting and destructive ideology is the strong anthropocentric (human-centered) view of creation; an idea, gathered from Genesis, that Gaia was given somehow to humans. "And God said unto them, 'Be fruitful, and multiply, and replenish the Earth, and subdue it: and have dominion over the fish of the sea, and over the fowl of the air, and over every living thing that moveth upon the Earth.'" (Genesis 1:28)

Much interest and debate over the role of the church in our attitudes towards Nature was sparked by the distinguished Professor of Medieval History at Princeton, Stanford and the University of California, Lynn White Jr. In late 1966, he gave a lecture to the American Association for the Advancement of Science (AAAS) entitled *The Historical Roots of Our Ecologic Crisis*. The lecture became well-known after it was published in the journal *Science* in 1967. White argued that there was a link between the theology of the medieval church and the 'exploitative' view of Nature starting in the medieval period. He blamed our current ecological crisis on the strong anthropocentric church doctrine and the church's elevation of 'man' (i.e. human beings) over and above Nature. This put the needs and aspirations of humankind ahead of those of the ecosystem and provided the foundation for the destructive attitude prevalent today that the Earth is simply a massive 'natural resource'. He also identified the close cooperation of the medieval church with the rise and development of technological invention. "What people do about their ecology depends on what they think about themselves in relation to things around them. Human ecology is deeply conditioned by beliefs about our nature and destiny – that is by religion." (White, 1967, pp. 1203-07) Regardless of what biblical scholars say about what this passage really means, people who read the Holy Bible find 'subdue it' and 'have dominion over' quite explicit. Claims that the ancient Holy Fathers actually meant something else, such as 'stewardship' seem to me to be lame and certainly have not diminished the effect this biblical injunction has had on Western attitudes towards Gaia.

In his landmark book, *The Ghost in the Machine*, Arthur Koestler writes extensively about what he calls the pathology of the human mind. In a chapter labeled, The Pathology of Devotion, Koestler suggests that remedies offered for the extensive human violence and cruelty over the last four thousand years by "Hebrew prophets, Greek philosophers, Indian mystics, Chinese sages, Christian preachers, French humanists, English utilitarians, German moralists, and American pragmatists" (p. 233) have had little effect. The reason he offers is that they were barking up the wrong tree. Blaming self-assertive tendencies of the individual such as selfishness and greed and appealing to our 'better nature' just hasn't worked. Instead, Koestler points to what he labels "the integrative tendencies of the individual" (Ibid) and cites examples such as human sacrifices to the Gods, torturing and burning of heretics, communist purges and gas chambers used to satisfy an urge for greater social good. Of course, in more recent history, we have had a more distinct example with so-called 'ethnic cleansing'. Koestler summarizes with: "The crimes of violence committed for selfish, personal motives are historically insignificant compared to those committed *ad majorem gloriam Dei*, out of a self-sacrificing devotion to a flag, a leader, a religious faith or a political conviction" (Ibid) and he suggests a kind of schizophrenia wherein: "Faith in a shared belief-system is based on an act of emotional commitment; it rejects doubt as something evil; it is a form of self-transcendence which demands the partial or total surrender of the critical faculties of the intellect, comparable to the hypnotic state." (p. 259) Whether a shift to an ecocentric worldview and realization that we as individuals emerged from a living, lovable and conscious being will alleviate human suffering despite the situation described above remains to be seen.

Can We Trash Our Home and Still go to Heaven?

Anne Primavesi reveals several important issues in her book *Gaia's Gift*. "Christianity has, as we have seen, exalted heaven at Earth's expense, literally, figuratively, and symbolically. This has meant that by consistently valuing eternal life after death (in heaven with God) above life on Earth, eternal life is made the goal of life on Earth." (Primavesi, 2003, p. 89) Our lives and all other living beings are thus systematically downgraded. When I was a child and pondered these mysteries from the bible, I remember wondering why we were not just born in heaven. Primavesi continues in this vein as she points out that Christianity's emphasis on heaven as a place where we go after death to dwell with God reveals another assumption. "This is that Earth is simply not good enough for us." And "it is certainly not good enough for God." Further: "A purely God-focused heaven ultimately discounts Earth as our natural home on the basis that God is not found here." (Ibid)

I suggest that it is cruel and tragic to teach the concept that we have a very brief Earthly existence followed by an eternity sitting at the right hand of God in a place thought of as heaven. These dark beliefs completely deaden any love and respect we might have acquired for our daily lives and our beautiful and bounteous planet. It beggars our logic and leaves us in a purposeless life waiting for some other worldly 'reward' while we commit ecocide with impunity. We find ourselves alienated from birth from the healing and sustaining energy of Gaia. Even Franz Kafka couldn't have come up with a more morbid thematic structure. At a recent funeral held in a Catholic Church, I heard the priest say: "Without the resurrection, life has no meaning." I had to restrain myself from jumping up with a challenge. Sitting quietly with that sentence ringing in my ears brought on a deep sadness and the agony of suppressed emotions. The recollection of the ending line from my favorite poem, *Requiem for Sonora*, by Richard Shelton, filled me briefly with despair: "But oh my desert: yours is the only death I cannot bear." With a God 'out there' somewhere holding a room for us when we die, why sacrifice for Gaia? No wonder so many of us watch our employers plunder our birthplace and say so little. After all, we are led to believe that we are only given temporary storage space here.

Disgraceful Ideologies such as Original Sin, Redemption and Eternal Damnation

There are no more harmful nor soul destroying ideologies in Christian culture than that of original sin. All who live within Gaia are born through love and within the freedom of an immense and powerful source of unconditional love, creativity and diversity. Any organization that teaches otherwise presents a dreadful danger to our mental health and well-being. Eternal damnation, the proposed need to somehow be somehow 'saved' or redeemed from guilt, and the idea that we are born in sin are the cruelest and most exploitative measures ever devised to keep church members in ignorance and bondage. We are all Earth beings; where else should we be? Mathew Fox puts it much more clearly in his book *Original Blessing*:

I believe that more patriarchal control, pessimism, anthropocentricism, and original sin ideology is profoundly dangerous and deviant. Dangerous for our planet and therefore for our children to come. And deviant for our souls that strive for hope and promise and creative co-creation.
(p. 5)

By the way, the concept of original sin came neither from the bible nor from the words of Christ. It was a political statement made by medieval thinkers in the early church.

By his sin Adam, as the first man, lost the original holiness and justice he had received from God, not only for himself but for all humans. Adam and Eve transmitted to their descendants human nature wounded by their own first sin and hence deprived of original holiness and justice; this deprivation is called 'original sin'. As a result of original sin, human nature is weakened in its powers, subject to ignorance, suffering and the domination of death, and inclined to sin (this inclination is called 'concupiscence').

Catechism of the Catholic Church, 416-418

I agree with Grace Blindell when she says:

It cannot be emphasized enough how widely this darkened view of original sin has cast its shadow. We all carry its scars whether Christian or not. Guilt, unworthiness, the rejection of the body as a source of sin, the suppression of spontaneous creativity, all these and more spring from this doctrine which has dominated our Western culture for centuries.

(Blindell, 2010, p. 31)

And further:

A spirituality that is centred in Creation looks to the real beginning, that cloud of shining incandescent radiance, the origin of all that now is. Fifteen billion years later a creation centered spirituality cannot look at the astonishing emergence of a self-aware form of life on this small planet and accept that this particular life-form is singled out to be born in sin.

(Ibid)

Apocalypse and Armageddon

Another seriously limiting belief comes also from the Holy Bible in the form of the belief in a second coming of Christ. Included in the New Testament we find: "For the Lord Himself will descend from heaven with a shout, with the voice of the archangel and with the trumpet of God, and the dead in Christ will rise first. Then we who are alive and remain will be caught up together with them in the clouds to meet the Lord in the air…" (Thessalonians 4:16-17). "The

Pale Horse causes pestilence and death from the sword, famine, plague and wild beasts and Hades follow it." (Book of Revelation 6:7-8) One quarter of the world's population die from the horsemen. There are thousands, maybe millions of people who believe that this event will occur very soon. Even worse, they feel no remorse over the destructive activities of humans and make no effort to diminish the damage. To me, this seems utterly sick. Wars and rumors of wars, floods and hurricanes, disease and death are welcomed as a sign that this coming is getting nearer. The basic belief is that this is destiny–God's will–and it will be done on Earth and heaven evidently. This material comes from Jewish history and is in no way related to the basic and inspired teachings of Jesus carried in the New Testament. Jesus of Nazareth made it very clear that God was a God of love.

Evolution or Creationism?

Charles Darwin delayed the publication of his thoughts on evolution until pushed by his good friend, Charles Lyell, when Darwin showed him a letter written by Alfred Russel Wallace detailing many of the same things Darwin himself was planning to publish. There can be little doubt that Darwin's hesitancy was caused by fear of a backlash by his critics and the church, mainly due to the implication that humans were directly descended from apes. Of course, his fears were realized. The professional and public outcry pointedly revealed the deep-seated belief in the society of those times (and which, unfortunately, still prevails today in many quarters) that humans were somehow outside of–and exempt from– the natural workings of Gaia. Anne Primavesi in her earlier book *Sacred Gaia* suggests to us four ways in which Christian theology "short-circuited evolutionary theory." The first of these holds that humankind is an exception to the way other beings came to be and, rather than evolving like every other life-form on Earth, was some sort of one time event within the last 6,000 years. The second assumes that our species is unique in that "God became a member of it" at a particular time. Thirdly, our species alone was "made in the image of God." And the fourth assumes that "we know our destiny, till the end of time, through divine revelation." (Primavesi, 2000, p. 37)

To this day, there is a huge following for Christian creationist theories advocating biblical explanations rather than scientific theories derived from scientific research. Young Earth Creationism is the most popular form of Creationism. For its adherents, a literal interpretation of the Holy Bible is the basis for their beliefs. They believe that the Earth is between 6,000 and 10,000 years old, that all life was created in six literal days, that death and decay came as a result of Adam & Eve's 'fall', and that geology must be interpreted in terms of Noah's Flood. According to a recent CBS poll, 55 percent of the American public does not believe in evolution. Another creationism belief, often referred to as Intelligent Design, is that the human genome is so irreducibly complex that it could not possibly have evolved. Unfortunately, American religious fundamentalism has a huge and growing influence on American politics and education; and obviously, for those people happily awaiting Armageddon, Gaia's health is not among the top ten items on their priority list.

Nature as Other—a Misleading Stereotype

Western culture has had a love-hate relationship with Nature. Any form of worship or spiritual belief running counter to–or even parallel with–church doctrine was labeled evil and sinful. "By absolutizing the difference between heaven and Earth, God is excluded from the world. In an allied move in the code, the difference between sacred and profane affects the desacralization of nature in order to specify religious rites alone as sacred." (Ibid, p. 67)

As we saw earlier, the power vacuum caused by the departure of the Romans from Gaul was partially filled by a resurgence of Pagan spirituality and a pantheism unacceptable to the church. Efforts to stamp out Pagan influence and practices reached their peak in the sixteenth century in Europe with the burning of witches, and persisted well into the late seventeenth century in the American colonies as illustrated by the Salem witch trials of 1692-93. Natural healing and herbal remedies, feelings and practices concerned with human kinship with Nature were associated with Paganism and those who were holding that energy and using that wisdom were generally put to death. Such is the paradoxical behavior of some who professed to worship the God of love. These events have taken their toll. It took until 2010 for Druidry to be re-designated as a religion in Britain and for census forms to be redrawn to count the Earth-based religions correctly. But their effects go much deeper than that. They have left us alienated from Nature such that we speak of Nature as 'out there' and 'other'. "Going out into Nature," we say, as though Nature were not within and around us and part of every cell in our bodies, intrinsic to our very being.

An Attitude of Respect

In this chapter I have been highly critical of the church as an institution and in its definitions of what God is and is not. Yet I honor and respect those individuals who feel that they must bear witness to spirit from within the churches and who maintain their loyalty towards the church hierarchy, no matter how flawed they may privately think it is. Their work is heartfelt and valuable. Reform from within is a difficult but very worthy task and I wish them every success. June Raymond, a sister of Notre Dame, explaining why she remains a Christian despite the negative and limiting things about the system, says: "It obviously is not because I love the institution. On the whole I don't, but the rest of it as well as its shadow is part of me and in this strange mystery of Christ I find my deepest being and a way back to the truths that transform and offer meaning and hope." (Raymond, 2010, p. 148) And in an interview with Michael Cohen, Rabbi Michael Lerner says:

> The God of the Bible is a God that says that the world can be based on love, that it can be based on caring–love your neighbor and love the stranger–that the world can go in that

direction, that that can happen. And not because of some transcendence of all that is but because the fundamental spiritual reality of the universe is that it is pervaded with love and goodness. And if you are a realized human being or moving in that direction, then your test is to be a witness to that possibility, to be a partner with God in the healing and transformation of the world. This is what it means to say that human beings are created in the image of God: We are meant to be partners, and our task is to actualize more of the goodness and love in the universe and to recognize the world as potentially transformable.

(Lerner, 2001, p. 2)

The Infallibility of Science—a Dangerous Belief

The scientific establishment has also hung on to some limiting beliefs. As pointed out in the previous chapter, a mechanistic scientific view treated the world as an orderly mechanical system with predictable outcomes explained through deductive reasoning. For instance, one of the crucial problems with climate change research is that we don't get people's attention with recent scientific findings because they lack certainty. Many people think science is talking about a dead machine. Our technological ability, as evidenced by moonwalks, atom smashers and spy satellites that can detect the color of our eyes from space, have lulled us into a sense of complacency. The thought is that a techno-fix can and will happen; it is just a matter of when and how much money will be needed.

Machines are not self-organizing. Once you study the prints and drawings of a machine, you may find out how it works and once you know how it works you can either fix or modify its operation. Complex organisms, like Gaia, don't reveal their inner workings by means of instruments used to measure mechanistic models. In addition, scientists find that the person making the measurement mysteriously affects the results. We are being doctored by university graduates who, for the most part, expect that medical science will come up for a fix for all the causes of human sickness. Again, it is just a matter of time and money. I have heard it said that there are not really more sick people, there are just more older people and older people are more likely to get sick. But no matter what the explanations, our technology has just not stopped the likes of cancer, heart disease, diabetes, and on and on mainly because our mechanistic attitude towards the human body enables 'Big Pharma' to dole out harmful pesticides, herbicides, sweeteners, and food additives with the left hand while with the right hand they try to convince physicians and the public that their newest drug will cure them – if they survive the side effects. I repeat, this deathly predicament is structured around a basic belief that the planet and its so-called occupants are mechanisms that can be understood and patched up, given enough time, effort and money.

As David Abram points out in his book *Becoming Animal*, too many scientists hold onto an assumption of complete objectivity. Research into quantum dimensions, axons, dendrites and black holes, for instance, go beyond our direct experience and the specifics are written in the made-up, theoretical language of scientific journals and academic papers. However, when it comes time to translate these papers into our everyday world language, these scientists are limited, just like any other person, by their "intuitions, expectations, proclivities, and perpetual habits borrowed from their ongoing (and taken-for-granted) engagement with the one realm that they inhabit with the whole of their animal bodies..." (Abram, 2010, p. 76). In other words, all scientific research findings are limited by the social/psychical filters embedded not only in their genetic makeup but determined by their very existence as an earthling.

Can Dysfunctional Basic Beliefs be Erased?

Basic beliefs are not all easily erased. But most can certainly be updated. For thousands of years, everyone believed that the Earth was flat, but eventually that belief gave way to a more accurate one as new information arrived. However, outdated beliefs can linger (as that one did, for a long, long time) if they are not consciously examined. And our feelings and actions can often be governed by outdated, unexamined beliefs of which we may be only barely conscious. So the first step is to become aware of a belief and recognize that it no longer fosters or aids your well-being or furthers your aims. How? It is possible, in a quiet moment, to search within by asking oneself: What do I believe about this or that subject? Where did this belief originate? Did I inherit it? How do I *really* feel about this? Is it still appropriate for me, now, in today's world? Keep going back and back until you find the source of the belief and then identify the feelings that surround it.

The second step is to re-program both your foundational belief and your mental picture of how you want to feel and act around the subject. You can change your belief, once you realize that it is dysfunctional, by substituting another one in its place. If you believe, for instance, that the Earth is strictly materiality and is composed of only rock of varying temperature with soil on top, you can substitute by planting, so to speak, the knowledge that the Earth is a living, conscious being of extraordinary intelligence and adaptability. Then you must visualize yourself acting out of that belief and in conjunction take a couple of initiating actions towards being that which you visualize. Visualization alone won't work and neither will only changing your actions. It takes the combination. Lastly, you must (a) practice staying aware of your thoughts and feelings so that you can pull yourself back when you digress into the old type thinking; and (b) practice seeing yourself as having already arrived at your goal. For instance, you might think, "I am grateful to be a part of this beautiful being that we call planet Earth or Gaia." Now to summarize, here is a short, easy to remember sequence of steps.

1. I am unhappy that I don't care about the welfare of our planet even though I realize that we need a healthy planet to maintain our personal health and well-being.

2. I have looked within and found out that I must have been taught and still believe that the Earth is only just molten lava within with water and soil on top.

3. I have replaced my early misinformation with the realization that our planet is a living, conscious being of extraordinary intelligence and adaptability that deserves my love and care and I want to learn to live in harmony with her rhythms.

4. I see myself now as a person that takes a keen interest in how the planet functions and have altered my living patterns to be in harmony with Nature insofar as reasonably possible and have started downsizing to lower my ecological footprint.

5. Each day I monitor my activities and avoid stepping back into old limiting thoughts and behavior patterns.

So how do we live? Is there a viable alternative to materialism and 'sky god' based religion? Yes there is. I suggest that we need to adopt what I call an 'Earthen Spirituality'. In the next chapter, we shall take a look at what an Earth-centered spirituality might look like.

At Fremington Quay

Wearing my band uniform, I am sitting on a too-hard chair on squelchy grass, near the quayside, my trombone heavy across my lap, brass gleaming in the sunshine. It rained hard this morning, but now it has stopped and I am enjoying the cumulus clouds floating majestically overhead. We have played several hymns. And now the Vicar is talking. He is telling us how grateful we should be to those who labored on the sea to bring us our goods, how dangerous it could be and how there would be a collection for the seafarer's charity. For today is Sea Sunday and we are gathered here to ask for blessings. Now it is the Methodist Minister's turn. The words of a long and ponderous prayer for God's blessing fade from my awareness as I look upwards again. Over a large expanse, not quite overhead and off to my left, there gleams a large, rounded area of high cirrus and that silky-patterned, windswept array that one so seldom sees. I feel tears coming into my eyes as I watch. Ranged around the horizon are the fluffy banks of cumulus, but here, in splendor for all to see, is Gaia's answer to the prayer. I gaze and I marvel as the scene quickly changes and the special display morphs into revolving fluffs. Yes, here is Gaia communicating and revealing that incredible loving force; free of charge and completely ecumenical, yet just in this moment. These revelations can sometimes last only a minute or two before they are wafted away forever by the wind. This exact view will never be repeated in measured time.

But who, besides me, is looking? Who else is receiving this true blessing? Gaia speaks, and speaks lovingly, but do we hear her? Do we see her? Her blessings are abundant but do we open to them? Do we hear the soft murmur of water over rocks; do we see the heart-stopping beauty of the sky or do we never look up? Can we smell the first breath of Spring and do we taste the sweetness of the small and delicate wild strawberry? If not, why not? Are we simply too busy?

5
What is Spirituality?

"A missionary once undertook to instruct a group of Indians in the truths of his holy religion. He told them of the creation of the earth in six days, and of the fall of our first parents by eating an apple. The courteous savages listened attentively and, after thanking him, one related in his turn a very ancient tradition concerning the origin of the maize. But the missionary plainly showed his disgust and disbelief, indignantly saying: 'What I delivered to you were sacred truths, but this that you tell me is mere fable and falsehood!' 'My brother,' gravely replied the offended Indian, 'it seems that you have not been well grounded in the rules of civility. You saw that we, who practice these rules, believed your stories; why, then, do you refuse to credit ours?"
Ohiyesa

"It is always easier to live in an illusive, but comfortable world, than in a true, but scary reality."
Vadim Zeland

"It is amazing that we should be so sensitive to suicide, homicide, and genocide and have absolutely no moral principles for dealing with biocide or geocide. Over-concerned with the well-being of the human, we feel it is better that everything is destroyed than that humans suffer to any degree."
Thomas Berry

Talking about spirituality is somewhat like talking about love. The word means something different to each one of us. The difficulty is that love and spirituality are not things that we have. They are not out there as objects to possess. They are a flow that we allow ourselves to become part of. Once we are fully part of that universal flow, we can never be separated from that which we love.

Defining Spirituality

One of the most difficult things about spirituality is defining it. As part of our mechanistic inheritance, often a definition is given more attention than the phenomenon to be defined. Then, of course, there are those rationalists who claim that if something cannot be weighed or measured it does not exist. I expect many of those who hold that belief love their parents, spouses and children. I would like to ask them: how large a container do you need to hold a pound of love? The explanation of what a definition is proposes that a definition describes a thing. Herein lies a major difficulty because spirituality is not a thing or object out there to be described. It is a way of being rather than something that we can have and hold. Another difficulty is that we have in our culture–most probably due to Christian church doctrine– made a dichotomy out of the term 'spirituality' by setting it over against 'worldliness', declaring some things sacred and others profane. As a result, spirituality has become further 'thingified'. And as a thing, spirituality can be lost, ignored, discarded or put on and off like an Easter Sunday hat.

In her excellent in-depth analysis of spirituality, Ursula King states: "It is perhaps more helpful to ask what spirituality does rather than what it is." (King, 2009, p. 3) My problem with the meaning of spirituality as offered in King's book is that it is so broad and all-encompassing that it could almost be summarized as 'the good'. Originally the word was mostly to do with our relationship with God and that which transcends our physical life on Earth. In later years, there came to be a crackerjack box of 'spiritualities' somewhat like the Zen of this and that. I rather like the following definition by Anna S. King:

> The term spirituality as currently used, indicates both the unity at the heart of religious traditions and the transformative inner depth or meaning of those traditions... It supplies a term which transcends particular religions and it suggests a non-reductionist understanding of human life.

It is more firmly associated than religion with creativity and imagination, with change, and with relationship. It is less associated in the popular mind with hierarchies of gender, race or culture. It indicates an engagement with or valuing of human experience and expression through art and music, through a response to nature and to ethical ideals as well as through the great religious traditions. It can embrace secular therapies and cosmologies as well as concerns with the environment. Thus it seems to include both sacred and secular, and to enable a fundamental rethinking of religious boundaries. Its very ambiguity and flexibility suggests a richness and texture which allows traditional religious maps to be redrawn and minorities to find a voice (and this also) makes it a more flexible concept than religion and encourages the user to reflect and to challenge institutionalized thought.
(King, 1996, p. 346)

In a paper presented at the Australian Association for Research in Education Conference, at the University of Melbourne in 2004, Brendan Hyde offers an extremely rich description of spirituality. He states that it "… is concerned with an individual's sense of connectedness and relationality with self, others, the world or universe, and with the Transcendent." (p. 3) Hyde cites Zohar and Marshall who understand spirituality to be holistic: There is a "dynamic wholeness of self in which the self is at one with itself and with the whole of creation." (Ibid, p. 4) Ursula King also points out that spirituality has a Christian context and had no direct equivalent in non-Western languages. Further she states that it is strongly connected with religion and appears to be opposed to splitting the two apart. Thus: "Such a sharp separation between spirituality and religion is not helpful for the development of the personal and social transformations so urgently needed if greater flourishing of humans and the Earth is to be achieved around the globe." (King, 2009, p. 2) My contention is just the opposite. I believe that the churches, as institutions, carry far too much baggage to be of much benefit to an Earth-centered spirituality – at least at this point in our cultural evolution. I agree with Thomas Berry when he says:

> I suggest we might give up the Bible for awhile, and put it on the shelf for perhaps twenty years. We need to experience the divine revelation presented to us in the natural world. The psalms do indeed tell us that the mountains and the birds praise God. But do we have to read the Scriptures to experience that?
>
> **(Berry & Clarke, 1991, p. 75)**

Goddess Spirituality

The idea of our Earth as female has emerged from the shadowy depths of history and has become embedded in our language as 'Mother Earth'. So it is not surprising that when we seek practitioners of Earthen Spirituality within our culture we find a deep resonance with the world-wide group of women who practice what they call Goddess Spirituality. One of their most well-known spokeswomen is Starhawk. As she says:

> Goddess religion is not based on belief, in history, in archaeology, in any Great Goddess past or present. Our spirituality is based on experience, on a direct relationship with the cycles of birth, growth, death and regeneration in nature and in human lives. We see the complex interwoven web of life as sacred, which is to say, real and important, worth protecting, worth taking a stand for. At a time when every major ecosystem on the planet is under assault, calling nature sacred is a radical act because it threatens the overriding value of profit that allows us to despoil the basic life support systems of the Earth.
>
> **(Starhawk, 2001, p. 1)**

Goddess spirituality is more comprehensive and less rigidly structured than the spirituality found associated with the major religions. It encourages creativity and spontaneity; relying on personal, internally focused power rather than institutional power. Groups work within various Pagan traditions that have retained the honor and respect for the Earth.

What is Earthen Spirituality?

Separation of the spiritual and the mundane does not exist under Earthen Spirituality. Even the distinction of whether this or that is more or less spiritual disappears and becomes meaningless. There is the awe of the world around us and the thankfulness and wonderment of just being. To separate our environment into dichotomies such as matter and spirit is simply eating out of the same old, grubby bowl of mechanistic, reductionist pap. I like the following expression from the *Hsin-Hsin Ming*, a poem written by Sengstan the third Chan Patriarch: "To set up what you like against what you dislike is the disease of the mind." There are many ways of looking at a tree, for instance. We can photograph it and note the color and texture of the bark. We can measure its height and circumference. With a saw, we can cut through it and note its hardness and reveal the beauty of its grain. None of these different ways of knowing the tree alters the fact that it is a whole, living organism.

Not being a Native American, I hesitate to bring up the subject of Native American spirituality for fear of misrepresenting or misinterpreting it due to my scant knowledge and experience and the fear that my generalizations might offend some who descend from a large population of numerous tribes. However, even from afar and as a descendent of those who largely destroyed Native American culture, I feel moved to point out what appears to me to be the practice of a profound Earthen Spirituality in the lives of many Native Americans. Followers of Native American spirituality do not regard their spiritual beliefs and practices as a 'religion' in the way that Christians do. Their beliefs and practices form an integral and seamless part of their very being. Furthermore, they do not think of themselves and the land as separate. I think it is fair to say that they consider private ownership of land as absurd. This deep connection gives rise to statements like, "You cannot separate us from the land because we *are* the land." To me, this is one of the most profound components of Earthen Spirituality. I suggest that the connection of those who love the land is not only physical but also a connection with the spirit of Gaia.

> We are the land. To the best of my understanding, that is the fundamental idea that permeates American Indian life; the land (Mother) and the people (mothers) are the same. As Luther Standing Bear has said of his Lakota people, "We are of the soil and the soil is of us." The Earth is the source and being of the people and we are equally the being of the Earth. The land is not really a place separate from ourselves, where we act out the drama of our isolate destinies... The Earth is not merely a source of survival, distant from the creatures it nourishes and from the spirit that breathes in us, nor is it to be considered an inert resource on which we draw in order to keep our ideological self-functioning... Rather for the American Indians... the Earth *is* being, as all creatures are also being: aware, palpable, intelligent, and alive... Many non-Indians believe that human beings possess the only form of intelligence in phenomenal existence (often in any form of existence). The more abstractionist and less intellectually vain Indian sees human intelligence as rising out of the very nature of being, which is of necessity intelligent in and of itself.
> **(Allen, 1989, p. 320)**

With an Earthen Spirituality, there are no 'houses of God'. Gaia's spirit is truly and thoroughly immanent. One has no need to 'go' anywhere to be with Gaia. In the words of a native Sioux, Ohiyesa:

There were no temples or shrines among us save those of nature. Being a natural man, the Indian was intensely poetical. He would deem it sacrilege to build a house for Him who may be met face to face in the mysterious, shadowy aisles of the primeval forest, or on the sunlit bosom of virgin prairies, upon dizzy spires and pinnacles of naked rock, and yonder in the jeweled vault of the night sky! He who enrobes Himself in filmy veils of cloud, there on the rim of the visible world where our Great-Grandfather Sun kindles his evening campfire, He who rides upon the rigorous wind of the north, or breathes forth His spirit upon aromatic southern airs, whose war-canoe is launched upon majestic rivers and inland seas – He needs no lesser cathedral!

(Eastman, 1911, p. 5)

Ursula King reminds us of the diversity of creation myths which reflected ancient cultural beliefs in a moral and cosmic order that extended beyond humans. "During modernity, many people have lost this integral vision, but it presents us with a deep spiritual intuition that needs to be reapportioned and become an essential part of a new ecological consciousness." (King, 2009, p. 147)

Yes, I suggest that our love of and respect for Gaia as a living, nurturing being fulfills this need. Earthen Spirituality, therefore, is not some 'New Age' impulse but a reapportioning or re-visioning of age-old beliefs into an ecological consciousness: one that we can embrace firmly, not only with love and thankfulness but with all our senses. In Earthen Spirituality there is no physical/spiritual split; we are a fully embedded, unified part of a cosmic holarchy that presents to our limited awareness a sense of systems within systems to an extent that is utterly beyond our imagination.

In her chapter of the anthology *GreenSpirit: Path to a New Consciousness*, Tania Dolley asks us to reclaim our animal bodies and reminds us of our connection to Gaia and "all there is." "Spirituality," she says, "is not about being 'above' the mere physical, human reality of our lives; rather, it is about embracing it, including and 'being with' all our experiences in a process of integration towards becoming a whole." (Dolley, 2010, p. 82)

Earthen Spirituality offers nothing in the way of answers to life's mysteries. Questions around the ultimate source of things, who created what from where and why are we here, can be placed in the box with other mysteries or left as a puzzle for our thinking function to work on. Perhaps they are mysteries only because our house of concepts lacks windows and access to the greater whole of which we are a part. We long for certainty and have been promised the certainty by establishment science. But the scientific method cannot keep its promise. Look back 500 years and recall that much of what was certainly true then has since then been rejected as false. The certainty of today may lead us seriously astray tomorrow. Surely we can learn to live quietly and cooperate fully with a life full of mystery? There need not be conflict, just calm and peaceful acceptance. Regardless of how we see or what we do not see, we can never be separated from that of which we are made. Each of us is an integral part of Gaia, the living, loving being.

Thinking Like a Planet

How might our ideas about various aspects of our existence change if we accepted that we were *in* a living, conscious planet rather than just *on* it? One of the most significant changes might be the elimination of the fear of death. I like the way Barbara Kingsolver puts it in her first book, *The Bean Trees*: "Although, when I thought about it (death) being dead seemed a lot like not being born yet, and I hadn't especially minded that." (p. 153) Let us re-examine what it is to die. All around us we can observe cyclical change; slow or fast or slight or radical change. When the changes that we call birth and death occur, the constituent physical parts that we call matter remain. So who dies? Certainly Gaia's consciousness does not die when a human dies. What if our thoughts and emotions are just as much a part of Gaia as our physical surroundings? As children many of us were taught that we have a spirit within us, coming in and then going out to either heaven or hell depending on a mysterious story about being 'saved' or not. That belief seems just as strange to me as my belief–that our minds are part of Gaia and thus we never 'die'– might seem to others. What if the greater part of our enlivening spirit never was inside our body? Looking at it in this way I ask, why would we need to go anywhere else?

Here again, we can use our recent scientific knowledge of quantum physics as a basis for making a hypotheses. We know that particles separated by huge distances are aware of each other's activities with no time lapse. There doesn't seem to be any 'out there' to quantum energy. What if every planetary bit of matter is enlivened to the extent that its evolutionary development permits? Let me use the example of a radio tuning mechanism which picks up a specific band of radio frequencies. The heart of the tuner is a variable tank circuit (a tank circuit captures and amplifies a particular frequency). The channel knob on the front of the radio with its moving vertical line over a series of numbers actually alters the capacitance of a tank circuit which in turn alters the resonant frequency or the frequency that is strengthened by the tank circuit. The output is then further amplified until voice or music emerges from the speaker(s). Perhaps there is a hierarchical progression of tank circuit abilities in all planetary objects and what we call life-forms have acquired more and more powerful circuits. Perhaps, as biologist Rupert Sheldrake has suggested, it is a question of what he calls morphogenetic fields (see Chapter 6). For instance, where in the body does consciousness reside? Where is the seat of the soul? I don't believe modern science has an answer to these questions. Perhaps answers have not been found because we are looking for them in the wrong place. Since consciousness isn't physical, maybe it resides outside and around the organism as a result of the organism's tuning capabilities, in the same way that the characters in a TV soap opera are not to be found living inside the TV set itself. It is possible that in a quantum field there is no time lapse and everything is actually happening at the same instant, the present moment. If so, then again, who dies? Of course, I am speculating, but is what I am suggesting any more speculative than the story of a soul rising out of the body at death and traveling to heaven to sit at the right hand side of God, forever? If we thought like a planet, would we still fear death in the same way? Our ideas of what happens after death have changed down through the ages. In ancient Egypt, only the pharaoh continued on to everlasting life. That's why the solid and sealed pyramids were filled with his belongings, food and other sustaining articles to keep him in the afterworld. Later, of course, it came to pass that all people could go to heaven. If what I have suggested above is true, then what is there to fear? Maybe we are looking for a science-based assurance. Maybe we are expecting to know ourselves as we truly are at the next hierarchical level with the mental capacities of a holon at our present level. Existence at the next level will always be a mystery. How would we survive if the organisms that make up our body became frozen with the fear of what their demise might hold for them and they stopped their cooperative activities? As I asserted above, we *are* the Earth. Where else would we go? In our ignorance we make a pejorative of cyclical change and feel the fear of death rather than the joy from the miracle of life.

6
Partnership of Science and Spirituality

"Thus, beyond the new science that glimmers a new worldview, we have a new view of God, not as transcendent, not as an agent, but as the very creativity of the universe itself. This God brings with it a sense of oneness, unity, with all of life, and our planet – it expands our consciousness and naturally seems to lead to an enhanced potential global ethic of wonder, awe, responsibility within the bounded limits of our capacity, for all of life and its home, the Earth, and beyond as we explore the Solar System."
Stuart A. Kauffman

"None of our religions have all the answers and even if we gathered the wisdom of all, that's not enough today. We have to bring in the wisdom of science and I would say yes, the wisdom of technology and even then we have to give birth to new forms of worship, to new forms of celebration, to new forms of forgiveness."
Matthew Fox

Through the eyes of Earthen Spirituality, science and spirituality are not split. Science grew out of two main features of the human psyche—wonderment and curiosity—that cause us to ask questions about the mystery of life. Curiosity is the trait which, from early infancy, prompts and enables us to learn about the world around us. We are all, by our very nature, interested in how other beings—human, animal and plant beings—work, and as we grow, our affinity and natural comradeship lead us to explore ways in which we might get to know these others better. Our curiosity about Gaia and how Gaia works is similar to the interest human lovers show in each other. There is that intense desire to get to know so the love may deepen. Wanting to learn more about how Gaia functions is a natural aspect of Earthen Spirituality. Western culture has called this 'science'. We recall our history and remember that science and spirituality parted company only around 500 years ago, mainly because of the restrictive policies of organized religion. Under Earthen Spirituality these two are again united.

A partnership between scientific research on the one hand and the deepening of spirituality on the other can play a huge role in our expanding consciousness of who we are in relationship to Gaia. Knowing Gaia as a living and loving being calls for a paradigm shift away from the traditional spirituality that focuses on the external divine and towards a path of reverence for the beauty and beingness of our Mother Earth. From this perspective, scientific research is a key resource, since it expands our awareness of just how this immense being functions. Modern science can thus be seen as the psychology of a planetary being. Seeing our planet as a living being, an integral part of a grand holarchy (see Arthur Koestler, *The Ghost in the Machine*) completely neutralizes what were once dichotomies, such as matter/energy, religious/secular and physical/spiritual.

As I explained briefly in Chapter 5, 'holarchy' is a far more accurate word than the better-known 'hierarchy' when it comes to understanding and describing how the universe appears to be ordered. Koestler explains that we have tended to define things as being either 'parts' or 'wholes' but this rigid dichotomy serves us poorly when we attempt to understand symbiosis and organisms, A deeper examination reveals that parts become wholes and those wholes become parts depending on where they fit within the system. Everything–except the entire universe–is a part of something else and everything is composed, in its turn, of parts. "Nothing in our known world–and certainly nothing on our planet–can exist as just a part or just a whole in an absolute sense." (Koestler, 1976, p. 48) Koestler called this phenomenon the 'Janus effect', taken from Janus who was a Roman God with two heads, one looking forward and one looking back. The Janus effect, he says, illustrates the dynamic of a holon. In all phenomena of life, there is the one face looking forward as a self-assertive part and back at an integrative whole. Diversity, uniqueness, symbiosis and the self-regulation properties of organisms at all levels are more easily understood through the looking glass of holarchies. Using holarchies rather than hierarchies as our ordering principle also protects us against the *hubris* to which humans have been so prone. In a hierarchy, the level of importance increases as you go up from small organisms to bigger ones, from the humble clerk to the powerful CEO. In a holarchy, importance works differently. Thus bees, earthworms and bacteria are revealed as being far more important to the continuance of healthy life on Earth than human beings are. Seeing it this way can provide a much-needed corrective to our way of thinking about what is referred to (as though it were simply a backdrop for human affairs) as 'the environment'. So as science progresses and discloses to us more and more of the wonderful and amazing processes of Nature, our awe and reverence for the mystery can only increase, bringing spirituality and science ever closer to each other.

Thomas Berry and Brian Swimme in *The Universe Story* have written a chapter calling for the end of the geological era termed the Cenozoic, which was characterized by a general cooling down of the planet and the growth of forests and development and proliferation of large mammals, and the beginning of what they call the Ecozoic era. This new era is characterized by "a new period of creativity participated in by the entire Earth community." (Berry & Swimme, 1992, p. 242) In this modern era, the Earth is recognized as an organic being and not seen as a collection of fragments that can be pulled apart and put back together like a picture puzzle. Earthen Spirituality is *the* spirituality that is appropriate for the Ecozoic era. There are many developments within the scientific and academic community leaning towards a less material reality and more to a position that emphasizes symbiosis and relationships. According to Ursula King, one of the most eminent academic writers in the field of environmental ethics, Holmes Rolston III, argues that "... contrary to the superficial impression that science might chase away the holy, we now discover that nature is mysteriously animated and inspirited." (King, 2009, p. 158) Brian Swimme suggests we find a way to contact the "primordial powers of the universe as they appear in the wind or in the flower or in the sunshine." He says, "Find a way to contact with the hope *simply of a moment of astonishment*. Maybe the role of the human depends upon such moments." (Swimme, 2010, p. 82) Brian speaks knowingly of an intelligent universe. He appreciates the elegance and intelligence revealed in the creation of 100,000,000,000 galaxies.

What follows is not meant to be a survey of the hundreds of scientists who are in tune with a holistic point of view, but just a few examples of how a study of Gaia from an organismic point of view can bring us into a deeper and more loving relationship with our precious planet. An excellent example is the work of biologist Lynn Margulis. Her brilliant and painstaking research reveals a serious flaw in Neo-Darwinian theory, with its questionable view of competition and strife as permeating the evolutionary history of Gaia. It is worth mentioning that, although Darwin's famous book is entitled *The Origin of Species*, almost nothing is actually explained concerning the beginnings of life and speciation. Darwin's writing was appropriate for his time and the state of the Establishment's scientific research doctrine of a mechanistic universe governed by an immutable law of Nature. Margulis maintains that Darwinism is excessively focused on inter-organismic competition. She speaks out for a much more cooperative relationship among species. In *The Symbiotic Planet*, Margulis claims that the fundamental fact of evolution is that all organisms large enough for us to see are composed of once-independent microbes teamed up to become larger wholes. As they merged, many lost what we in retrospect recognized as their former individuality and performed their former function within the context of the next higher holon. She has shown that many of the constituent parts of cells today still exist as individuals, betraying their origins as the independent organisms that they were, many millions of years ago. In fact, all higher organisms are composed of a gathering together of lower functional organisms in a vast cooperative venture rather than as the result of chance mutation. For example, the flatworm *Convoluta Roscoffensis* is transparent and green because of algae that live, grow and die within its body. *Convoluta* feeds off the by-products of photosynthesizing action of the algae. It is hard to see where the animal ends and the algae begin. The flatworm's mouth does not function after the larvae hatch. The algae also recycle the worm's uric acid into food for themselves. Her theory is named SET or Serial Endosymbiosis Theory and is widely accepted by mainstream scientists. Why is this change in evolutionary theory important? The pattern of symbiosis found in cells and higher organisms–the human body being perhaps the most advanced–rather than random mutation falls more in line with systems theory where organisms cooperate for their mutual well-being. It is easier to love a world where cooperation prevails than one ruled entirely by competition.

Quantum Mechanics Rips Holes in Newtonian Scientific Certainty

Quantum theory brings up a huge challenge to our worldview and common understanding of the nature of our reality. Even a rough explanation of Quantum mechanics and systems theory is beyond the scope of this book. Nevertheless, there are some parts of quantum theory that even a non-physicist can grasp if the phenomena are presented clearly as Fritjof Capra demonstrated with his fascinating and informative book, *The Web of Life*. Werner Heisenberg, a Nobel Prize winner in 1932 and professor of theoretical physics at the University of Leipzig, formulated one of the cornerstones of quantum mechanics, the Uncertainty Principle. This signals a major departure from Newtonian physics, as it seriously questions the 'little round balls' explanation of Newtonian matter. Simply stated, one cannot accurately measure both the momentum and position of a quantum particle at the same time. Quantum physics researchers agreed to describe movement of minute quantities–quanta–in terms of both particles and waves because neither Newtonian definition served fully to describe quanta as one or the other. It's a matter of 'both/and' rather than 'either/or'.

Another eminent physicist, John Bell, asserts with Bell's Theorem (an expression of the Einstein-Podolsky-Rosen paradox) that when two particles interact and then go their separate ways, any subsequent disturbance with one particle will instantly affect the other one, regardless of the distance between them. They behave as one without the use of messages or 'hidden variables'. These findings turn our notions of precise 'locality' inside out and call for a new way of looking at the world around us. Heisenberg, Bell and many others over a period of years showed us that our world is stranger than we can ever imagine. Science got so caught up with looking for fundamental building blocks that most researchers overlooked the fact that they were perhaps basing their research on false premises. The Universe seems to be made up of energetic relationships rather than distinct particles. Perhaps the most interesting systems theory so far is that of Geoffrey Chew in his Bootstrap Philosophy. He has been professor of physics at the UC Berkeley since 1957. His theory denies any fundamental entities whatsoever and in the words of Capra: "The material universe is seen as a dynamic web of interrelated events. None of the properties of any part of this web is fundamental; they all follow from the properties of the other parts, and the overall consistency of their interrelations determines the structure of the entire web." (Capra, 1996, p. 39) The implications of this theory are profound and lead us, as with uncertainty and locality, to a new way of thinking about the nature of Gaia and how she, as a living being, might operate.

The New Biology

Few people realize just how powerful our basic beliefs can be; especially the limiting and destructive ones that I alluded to in Chapter 4 where I cited the cell biologist Bruce Lipton. Lipton tells a healing story that illustrates the power of the mind. In the early 1950s, a British physician successfully cured what he thought was a very bad case of warts by using only hypnosis. It was only after taking his patient to the referring surgeon that he was told he had made a mistake. The patient actually had an incurable disease caused by a congenital disorder called ichthyosis. It seems that unconditional belief in the healing power is essential for success. The medical doctor was probably unable to replicate his success because of his admitted doubt that he could again cure incurable illness. Although he pretended that he believed, he later admitted that he was acting. Is there a scientifically sound explanation for the phenomenon described above? Lipton thinks so and he finds the key in quantum physics that reveals the extent to which matter and energy are entangled. He remarks, "Thoughts, the mind's energy, directly influence how the physical brain controls the body's physiology." (Lipton, 2005, p. 125) According to Lipton, thoughts can change each cell's function–producing proteins by sending signals that favor a particular protein combination. Even after the genius of Albert Einstein plus the deepening knowledge of quantum physics over the last 60 years, the mind-body split in Western medicine tragically still prevails. Further research similar to Bruce Lipton's may reveal that Gaia transmits a frequency that sustains all earthly beings proportional to their ability to resonate with it. Perhaps we disconnect and allow ourselves to be alienated to our great peril.

The Plant Kingdom

The study of Gaia as a living organism has been in progress for many years. Great strides have been made in the study of ancient plant life and its development. There has been a synthesis arising "out of the seamless integration of new knowledge concerning the physiological and ecological behavior of living plants and ecosystems into the subject of Palaeobotany." (Beerling, 2007, p. 198) In his book *The Emerald Planet*, David Beerling explains how the integration of plant physiology into Palaeobiology allows fossil plants to act as tachometers of Earth's history. He points out how plants themselves can actually be geological forces of nature. By searching fossil records for conditions similar to what we have now, one can more accurately predict our near future. For example, in the carbon rich atmosphere of over 350 million years ago, plants had no leaves and very few stomata (stomata are pores on the surface of land plants). Genetically, they were prepared to develop leaves, but they did not. Somewhere between 400 and 350 million years ago the planet's CO_2 content dropped by 90 percent. Temperature also fell and an ice age gripped the polar and sub-polar regions. A few million years later, tree leaves evolved with considerable numbers of stomata, which they use to absorb CO_2. The theory is that since stomata also serve to release moisture, there needed to be fewer in number in a hot climate. In the cooler environment, more stomata could be utilized to gather up the scarcer CO_2. The fact that leaves in the South of England have lost 40 percent of their stomata in 150 years correlates with the increase in CO_2 and is an example of how the past records help us to understand the present. One of Beerling's two objectives in writing his book was to illustrate how plants not only react to their environment but also change their environment in ways that enhance their well-being. Of course, this is an important aspect of the Gaia Theory.

Animate Earth

For a substantially complete story of how earthly beings help alter their environment, see *Animate Earth* by Stephan Harding. One of my favorite sections in this book is where Harding explains how forests stimulate the moisture formation they require in two ways. One, they alter the albedo by developing lighter color when they want to reflect more sunlight; and two, they affect rainfall by taking up carbonyl sulfide (COS) and then releasing dimethylsulfide (DMS) which seeds planet-cooling clouds. (Harding, 2006, p. 131) The chapter, 'Carbon Journeys', conveys a fascinating picture of the carbon cycle and the role of calcium and plants in breaking out carbon from the air.

Gaia and Evolution

In the book *A New Science of Life*, Rupert Sheldrake introduces his Hypothesis of Formative Causation which, in a few words, suggests that morphogenetic fields control repetitive forms of living organisms. "They impose patterned restrictions on the energetically possible outcomes of physical processes." (1981, p. 13) Towards the end of the book, Rupert sets out four different metaphysical theories that are compatible with his hypothesis. One of them he calls The Conscious Self. This theory suggests that the body may have motor fields controlling movement functions in organs such as the gut, the heart and lungs. Motor fields keep the organism closely connected with itself and its environment. Conscious memories, for example, may be stored outside the body. Here, one is reminded of Jung's collective unconscious. Further, this phenomenon could also shed light on various "parapsychological phenomena which are inexplicable in terms of energetic or of formative causation." (Ibid, p. 203)

Quantum Coherence

Mae-Wan Ho is a retired scientist with experience in Biology, Biochemistry, Biophysics and Genetics. She is the founder and Director of the Institute of Science in Society which is a non-profit organization devoted to providing critical and accessible scientific information to the public and to promoting social accountability and ecological sustainability in science. One of Mae-Wan Ho's serious interests and one of her research subjects is the principle of quantum coherence. She has stated in an article published in the Institute of Science and Society, Kybernetes 26, 265-276, 1997: "I propose that quantum coherence is the basis of living organization and can also account for key features of conscious experience– the 'unity of intentionality', our inner identity of the singular 'I', the simultaneous binding and segmentation of features in the perceptive act, the distributed, holographic nature of memory, and the distinctive quality of each experienced occasion."

Coherence, as you would expect, means that a group of substances 'stick' together. Mae-Wan Ho, as I understand, theorizes that from a cellular scale on up to perhaps the universe, the various parts making up an organism work together, synchronize or phase-lock their activities in a huge cooperative undertaking, yet maintain their private integrity. Further, the organism is thick with coherent activities at all levels, which are coordinated in a continuum from the macroscopic to the molecular. The organism really has no preferred levels. That is the essence of the coherent organic whole, where local and global, part and whole are mutually implicated at any time and for all times.
(Ho, 2008, p. 221)

In 1989 she stated: "Human consciousness may have its most significant role in the development and creative expression of the collective consciousness of nature." (Ho, 1989, p. 10)

One of Ho's most amazing discoveries was the brilliant interference colors caught by an unconventional use of a polarizing microscope trained on some Drosophila (fly) larva. These types of images were formerly restricted to rock crystals and tell us about long range order in arrays of molecules and reflect their liquid crystal property. Another of her interests and research subjects is the amazing properties of water. Recent research in structured water reveals how electric charges are passed along by water molecules. It appears that all the cells in the body are mechanically and electrically interconnected by connective tissue (skin, bones, cartilage, tendons, veins, air passages etc). Parallel research has verified the existence of crystal cell structure and holographic memory retention properties. "Memory of the brain-body is distributed over the entire liquid crystalline medium." (Ibid, p. 240) In other studies she focuses on bio-photon light emissions and the probability that they may enable long distance communication. All this research activity can be interpreted with a holistic bias which reveals a quantum world where every entity is fully connected and evolves like an organism.

Life-Forms are the Nerve Endings of Gaia

Gaia may supply the motor fields theorized by Sheldrake as part of the evolutionary development of the diversity of what we call life. These fields along with other developments that our scientific instruments cannot detect may enable all the bits of Gaia to express, in a two-way circuit, Gaia consciousness. It doesn't seem so far out to me that we and our brother and sister life-forms are the nerve endings of Gaia; the means for Gaia to be conscious of herself. The following quote from Primavesi provides a good conclusion to this chapter:

> If theology is to express contemporary truth today, it will intersect somewhere with the metaphorical networks of science. As the 'eternal verities' are put in question by new knowledge, new truths are introduced into the universe. New theological descriptions must, then, also emerge.
> (2000, p. 45)

The Flame Robin

There is just an indirect hint of dusk since the sun lowered itself behind the hill over an hour ago. As I look out over the small valley stretched out below me a soft murmur of a strong but gentle wind draws my eyes expectantly up and to my right along the distant eucalyptus-lined hillside. Very soon, along the ridge, leaves begin to tumble and quake until, like a wave approaching the shore, a sighing, invisible column of air makes its way along and down through the gully, ruffling leaves and becoming louder as it moves. And then all is quiet and still again. I can't explain why this scene, this momentary passage of breeze through one little gully, holds so much fascination for me. I know there is a message there from Gaia, but I lack the ability to comprehend it.

I cross my legs and resume my idle gaze out along the valley before me. Suddenly, a flame robin alights on the toe of my boot. The Australian flame robin exhibits the same qualities of stillness and stealth as flycatchers do: that same intent peering ahead for prey. Watching these little birds is one of my favorite pastimes. I have often noticed that no sooner do I pound in another garden stake and walk away then… zoom! A robin alights on it. But to have this beautiful little being choose my upturned boot as a perch nearly stops my heart. I realize I am holding my breath. The pleasure of being so near and in a strange way intimate with a wild creature of the air invokes a feeling of privilege. I feel honored by such a presence. Soon, the robin flies down to peck at something and then on to a garden fence post. Of course, to the robin, I am just another elevated stick. So the pleasure is all mine.

7
Earthen Spirituality Practice

"Practicing Nature means being in tune with her rhythms. She instructs: Notice the phase of the Moon. Day by day see her movement across the sky. Notice from month to month how she rises later or earlier. What is her position in the sky? Watch the birds as they pass through on their journeys southward or northward. Who lingers longest? Listen to the squirrels. Notice colors of trees and plants and sky. Learn Autumn. Learn Winter. Learn Spring. Learn Summer. Tune into her. Feel your connection to her. Adore her. That is the beginning of the practice of Nature."

Diane Wolverton

There are two main kinds of spiritual practice: communal and individual. Communal spiritual practices are culturally derived and thus vary geographically even within the same creed or religion. Sometimes, religions and spiritual practices cross-fertilize and give birth to new forms. A good example of this is the way Buddhism, when it migrated from India to China in 530 AD, met and melded with Taoism to form *Chan*. Which, when it was transmitted from China to Japan around 1000 AD, took on the flavor of Japanese culture and became Zen. Another example is the Folk Christianity that was practiced in medieval England and Ireland. Although unity was not achieved among the Irish and other Celtic peoples, ethnic customs survived the edicts of Roman Catholicism.

Spiritual practices honoring the Earth will thus differ from place to place, region to region and culture to culture. And of course from climate to climate, since they are linked to the Earth's turning circle. The closer places are to the poles, the more likely we are to find celebrations that honor four clearly defined seasons, marked by the solstices and equinoxes and the various points in between. Many of the Celtic festivals were co-opted by Christianity, such as the absorption of Yule by Christmas and the overshadowing of Samhain by All Souls' Day and its modern eclipse by a highly commercialized Halloween. Yet the ancient meanings shine through. For all the ingredients are still there, thinly disguised. The Christian Easter may not be celebrated in quite such earthy ways as the fertility festivals of old, but its symbols of fertility–the egg and the notoriously fecund rabbit–are just as obvious.

Yule, as we know, was the Celtic festival of the winter solstice, marking the moment of deepest dark and the first tiny turning towards the light. Notice how that same feeling of turning towards the light is expressed in numerous ways by our Christmas traditions – candles, fairy lights, twinkling tinsel, cards and cakes with sparkling, white frost on them… and so on. The songs and stories may be different–though even there, the old influences can be easily discerned–but the deeper impulse is unchanged.

Communal, spiritual practices have two aspects–the outward sign and the inward significance. Every ritual action is what Christians like to call 'the outward, visible sign of an inward, spiritual grace'. Vast numbers of people in our secular Western culture take part in these more recent forms of what were once Earth-based, communal, seasonal rituals. And because, as we have seen, the archetypal energies of these seasonal rituals are so strong, it is possible for many of us to reassign the inward meanings of these shared rituals in ways that enable us to honor and celebrate Gaia and her seasons, just as our ancestors did. We can ceremonially mark the solstice as we switch on the tree lights and give thanks to Gaia as we eat our Christmas dinner.

The Sharing of Food
The solstice is not the only moment in the calendar that is marked by feasting. The ritual of sharing food has been used by many cultures as a means of showing honor and respect, especially to visitors. Some groups ritually use eating to reground themselves after a spiritual 'high'. In addition, sharing a meal fosters communion

among group members, especially when blessings are included. Turning food into a commodity for sale was a tragic result of the shift from a hunter/gatherer to an agricultural society. Every Earth being has an inalienable birthright to participate in the nutrient passing, life-sustaining natural ritual of eating. The sharing of food is a fundamental Earthen Spirituality ritual.

> The magic and sacrament of Food – The Loving Cook turns every aspect of her life into a mindful, prayerful, practice. She's ever conscious of the source of our food, gives thanks with every breath to the fertile, hallowed ground. Thanks to God, to Gaia, to the Holy Spirit in any language, by any name. She understands that the quality of 'holiness' is related to 'wholeness': being complete, coherent, connected through spirit to all that is.
> **(Hardin, 2004, p. 159)**

Rituals around food, such as the saying of grace before meals, the blessing of the food or a silent, mindful meditation before eating are extremely important as memory-joggers for thankfulness. They remind us to be thankful for our aliveness and for the reciprocity of love between ourselves and Gaia.

As well as the community-wide rituals that honor Nature around us, there are also important moments when we pause to honor and celebrate Nature as it flows within and through us and our families. Birth, naming, the first step, the first word, puberty, betrothal, pregnancy, lactation, menopause, illness, healing, death, burial – all of these and more are part of our celebration of the aliveness of our bodies. They are our own, personal seasons and these, too, we celebrate communally, as and when the need arises.

Earthen Spirituality, however, is something that can be practiced individually as well as communally and not just at special times but from moment to moment.

Individual Practice

In most spiritual traditions, there are practices that the individual follows in private. Saying one's prayers, saying affirmations, setting up a personal shrine or altar at home, displaying art objects with symbolic, spiritual meaning, fasting, journaling, vision quest or pilgrimage, body-based regimes such as Yoga or Tai Chi, the wearing of symbols and amulets, the saying, singing or chanting of special sounds and phrases, the casting of oracles… all these are examples of personal, spiritual practice. Just as all these practices exist, in some form or another, in every spiritual tradition, likewise all can have their equivalence in the personal practice of Earthen Spirituality. It is up to each individual to bring his or her chosen practices into being in everyday life, in whatever form feels appropriate or desirable and has the most personal meaning.

The Quiet Mind

The fundamental personal practice, which cuts across many spiritual traditions, is self-knowledge. Not just understanding our surface personalities and characteristics but making contact with that deeper aspect of ourselves that Jung referred to as the Self, with a capital 'S'. A prerequisite for reaching the Self is what is often referred to as quieting the mind. Most of us realize that our thinking function is constantly chattering away. That need not be a problem in itself, but too often we get caught up in the chatter and lose awareness of sensations and feelings that our bodies are constantly picking up. Our thinking function deals strictly with concept; so when we allow ourselves to be almost completely absorbed in this head traffic, we have blocked our connection with the real world around us. Many people find meditation very helpful in calming down and avoiding getting caught up with the flow of thoughts.

One meditation practice that is simple to describe yet incredibly difficult to follow is the art of just *being* rather than doing or becoming or thinking about doing or becoming. Instead of using a concentration-based method such as sitting and concentrating on your breath or an object or mantra, you do the opposite. Rather than allowing yourself to focus on any particular object you try to remain open and keenly aware of *everything*, but without any attachment to anything. You notice all sensory impressions. It is like standing at a bus stop, watching buses roll by but not catching any of them. The trick is to not get caught up in thinking function analysis or judgment. An itch, for instance, is not thought of as a problem; there is just the itch and the present moment. Instead of, "Oh dear, my leg is itching!" there is just the basic awareness of an itch. For some people, there is a subtle shift that results from lots of practice. What may have begun as focusing on observing all that was coming in changes to just 'being with' it all. The distinction of being with yourself and what you believe is 'out there' dissolves into a 'there just is' beingness. Perhaps this is what some people mean by 'oneness'.

If we get caught up in our thinking function we only experience concepts of what we see, hear and feel etc. We then live in a whole world of concepts rather than the true world of embeddedness in the Earth. For example, most of us have from time to time anticipated fear of an event that hasn't actually happened. We visualize and anticipate *in concept* the disaster that brings forth the real fear and suffering over an event that may never actually happen. The body prepares for this threat with the 'fight or flight' response, including the release of adrenaline, which we sometimes work through by picking a fight with our spouse, children or friends. Then we get stressed by guilt and remorse for how we have reacted which then often turns into depression. When the mind gets depressed, the body shuts down its receptors to the sustaining love and care emanating from Gaia and we fall prey to apathy. What often follows is despair which invites and sustains the dark energy some call evil. We search in vain for happiness; not understanding. As Francis Lucille puts it: "The ego can only understand happiness objectively, as a state to be obtained in the future." (Lucille, 2009, p. 102) Unfortunately tomorrow just never comes.

There are probably as many different meditation methods as there are people who meditate. But to generalize, one could say that, regardless of the method, meditation appears whenever we are not in our thoughts but in quiet listening; *being with* whatever is going on in and around our body. In the words of Krishnamurti:

> So when we use the word 'meditation' we do not mean something that is practiced. We have no method. Meditation means awareness: to be aware of what you are doing, what you are thinking, what you are feeling. Aware without any choice to observe to learn. Out of this awareness comes attention – the capacity to be completely attentive. Then there is freedom to see things as they actually are without distortion.
> **(Krishnamurti, 1969, p.80)**

Thich Nhat Hanh, a Buddhist monk, associates meditation with mindfulness and mindfulness with peace. "Some people think there is a difference between mindfulness and meditation, but this is not correct. The practice of mindfulness is simply to bring awareness into each moment of our lives... The time you spend washing dishes and doing all your everyday tasks is precious. It is a time for being alive. When you practice mindful living, peace will bloom during your daily activities." (Hanh, 2003, p. 5) The point is that we be 'in the moment', not *thinking about* the moment. Be fully absorbed in the action with the accompanying sensations without engaging the thinking function. Of course, the ego – the thinking function–will resist mightily, even desperately, because it can only function when you leave your native presence and allow it to take over. Descartes did have it wrong by the way. We are not our thinking function. However, don't fight with your ego: love and appreciate it. Just give your ego the gift of rest. Assure your ego that you will call on it when an analysis is desired. Under an ecocentered existence, meditation need not be ritualistic as something special that you schedule and perform from time to time. The benefits of meditation can be available in each waking moment.

As people turn their attention to the rhythms of Gaia, I believe that more and more Earthen Spirituality rituals, both personal and communal, will emerge from the utter delight in observing Nature. Ancient observances that have survived the centuries will be rediscovered and welcomed back into our lives and many new, modern, rituals will develop in time as people replace the empty rituals of consumerism with meaningful ways of celebrating our earthly existence. We are moving into a new era of creativity, this time in partnership with Gaia and in full awareness, for the first time, of her true nature–and our own.

8
Can We Be Full Partners with Gaia?

"We abuse land because we regard it as a commodity belonging to us. When we see land as a community to which we belong, we may begin to use it with love and respect."
Aldo Leopold

"We cannot win this battle to save species and environments without forging an emotional bond between ourselves and nature as well – for we will not fight to save what we do not love."
Stephen Jay Gould

"The Moment we begin to fear the opinions of others and hesitate to tell the truth that is in us, and from motives of policy are silent when we should speak, the divine floods of light and life no longer flow into our souls."
Elizabeth Cady Stanton

Delicate Balance

Perhaps too late we have come to understand that the behavior patterns of Gaia, a living being, are not as precise as the mathematical formulae and models we have built up to predict a machine's behavior. Newtonian physics and the mechanistic model of physical reality dominate our thinking, primarily due to an educational system that is slow to accept new scientific discoveries and to honor new theories and their implications. Gaia as an organism can be better understood through a holistic outlook wherein the planet is an aggregate which includes a complex set of relationships with its various parts. We often encounter difficulty in explaining the implications of holism because so much of the accepted language we use emerged out of the mechanistic paradigm. Rational, Establishment science chose the game and the rules. However, when scientific data fail to describe an aspect of reality according to the accepted rules, they are deemed unreliable and tossed out. The peer review procedures are written by those who made up the rules of the game so that incoming evidence which fails to conform to the rules is also tossed out. In this way, a healthy evolution of theory is short-circuited. Of course, so much scientific research is now paid for by multinational corporations that science has become, in many instances, a tool of the marketplace.

We are a very Powerful Part of Nature

Since we are part of Nature, then isn't what we do natural too? Yes, of course. However, we are the first beings spawned by Gaia who can significantly affect Gaia's survival structures and cycles. What bacteria took millions of years to accomplish, we can destroy in a lifetime. We are the first Earth beings, as far as we know, who have figured out how to survive as we eat out our environment. No other animal settles male rivalry issues by purposely fighting to the death. We have not learned to control our numbers like most other animals. As several wise elders have pointed out, especially Brian Swimme and the late Thomas Berry, we are now–and not by our conscious choice–co-creators with Gaia of our environment. Unfortunately, we are not ready to assume such power and neither have we yet demonstrated the wisdom necessary for such an awesome undertaking. Neither is it, in my opinion, reasonable or probable, as Thomas Berry suggested, that the appearance of humans is "the moment in which the unfolding Universe becomes conscious of itself." (Berry, 1988, p. 132)

Berry's statement above appears to echo Tielhard de Chardin who put forth a similar thought. In the words of former editor of *Creation Spirituality* magazine, John Mabry: "In Teilhard's estimation, humankind is the crowning achievement of the universe, because it is in us, and, as far as we yet know, only in us, that the Creation has become self-aware." (Mabry, 1994) I believe that the crow, for instance, that was filmed using three different sizes of stick in a particular order to obtain food was aware of what it was doing. What about whales and dolphins? We really don't have any way of ruling them out. Where *Homo sapiens* stand in the possible hierarchy of universal life-forms is beyond my comprehension. As I have said before, my suggestions for a modified vision stop with our life within Gaia.

Gaia—an Intelligent Planet

Our Establishment scientists and religious leaders are still unable to grasp the significance and import of the growing weight of evidence that we are an outgrowth of a living, loving being–a being with the intelligence and ability to self-regulate. We assume that our lovely planet is dumb and that what we see and measure is some chance combination of physical forces that work as cause and effect in a mechanistic paradigm. How about asking: why do we now have a ratio of nearly 90 percent cooling and only a little over 10 percent warming over an expanse of around 125,000 years? Millions of years ago there was a lot more CO_2 in the air, it was much warmer, and the oceans were far more expansive than now. Could it be that this oscillation of cooling periods with shorter warming periods is necessary to self-regulate us towards maintaining a livable environment? We must remember that Gaia acts, in comparison to our lifespan, in significantly longer-term increments. We know that the sun's output of heat and energy is expanding. Stars that astronomers have studied have a life cycle of expanding energy until they become red giants then and spurt out planetary material. This knowledge led James Lovelock to question why the Earth was not hotter. One result was the Gaia Hypothesis which is now a full-blown Gaia Theory.

Go with the Flow

In the past millennia, creatures, warm and cold-blooded beings, plant and mineral beings exercised their innate drive to expand their activity and awareness. It is only now that our species has pushed the envelope to an extent that we must use the combination of our thinking function and our deep intuitive knowing to make wise decisions. With power comes responsibility. We have the science, we have the spirituality, we potentially have the wisdom and we have the level of consciousness to not only survive, but share in the increasing health of Gaia. Yes, there are detractors, there are greedy people and corporations without moral sensitivity, but they cannot prevail over the loving grace of Gaia. As we become ever more conscious, our understanding will grow and our feeling of connectedness will deepen. The power of Gaia's love as it is expressed in us is wondrous and beyond imagination. "If the extinction of humans ever happens, it will be because we neglected to respond to her (Gaia) 'feelers' and healers, failed to fulfill our Gaian and evolutionary role." (Hardin, 2004, p. 128) The appeal I am making to the reader is just to stop and think about a possible alternative in the way we look at our planet. Please start questioning your suppositions as to just what it means to be a part of a living planet.

Gaia is a philosophical agent with great freedom as a being to express herself. One can look upon Gaia as she manifests or mediates the creative energy of the cosmos. Let us not get caught up in disputes about the details of the mechanism used by the Cosmos to impart this creativity. We are just not in a position to pronounce on just how this is done. Why argue over whether it is a kind of radiation from a divine source outside or whether it is an emergent phenomenon? There are endless debates and a vocabulary of distinctiveness, for example, around pantheism (God is everything), or panentheism (everything is in God). People obtain doctorates in philosophy running this distinction around and around. Let me put it this way: take yourself away from streetlights and light from cities–if you can find such a place anymore–on a clear, new moon night and just lie back on the ground and gaze out through the Milky Way, our galaxy. Try counting the visible stars and remember that the fuzzy bits and globs you see are countless stars and millions of galaxies. Now then start telling us about the nature of God, the Creator. How are you going to write 60,000 words on that?

We just don't know much at all about the universe or cosmic energy or forces. For example: "It seems that ordinary matter–gas, stars, planets and galaxies– makes up less than five percent of the Universe. The remainder is unseen. Astronomers believe that 70 percent of this is 'dark energy'–a hypothetical phenomenon that affects the rate at which the Universe expands. The remaining 25 percent is believed to be dark matter." (Gill, 2009) I suggest that the most brilliant of our scientists don't really know, although they describe attributes, what gravity really *is*. We can hardly begin to understand what we can see and measure let alone the purely theoretical stuff that we can't see. I am not implying that we should not ponder the mystery of life. I personally enjoy it. But to place such importance on this effort that we spend endless days and months disputing while ignoring the effect our species is having on our birthplace, our habitat, our greater selves is a kind of madness. Why not accept, now, in this present moment, the mystery, and become fully embedded in your birthright, grounded in your beingness, and fully engaged with the beauty and nurturing aspect of Gaia.

References

Abram D. (2010), *Becoming Animal*, Pantheon Books, New York

Allen, P.G. (1986), *The Sacred Hoop*, Beacon Press, Boston, in (1989) *Weaving the Visions*, Christ, C. and Plaskow, J. (Eds.), Harper Collins, San Francisco

Bateson, G. (1979), *Mind and Nature: A Necessary Unity*, Hampton Press, NJ

Beerling, D. (2007), *The Emerald Planet*, Oxford University Press, Oxford, NY

Berger, A., Loutre, M. (2002), "Climate: An exceptionally long interglacial ahead?" *Science* 297 (5585): 1287-1288

Berry, T., Clarke, T. (1991), *Befriending the Earth*, Twenty-Third Publications, New London, CT, USA

Berry, T., Swimme, B. (1992), *The Universe Story*, HarperOne, NY

Blindell, G. (2010), "Seeing Things Differently", in McCain, M. (Ed.), *GreenSpirit: Path to a New Consciousness*, O Books, Hants, UK

Blindell, G. (2001), *What is Creation Centred Spirituality* (online), http://www.greenspirit.org.uk/resources/GraceB.htm (Accessed 20 December 2010)

Capra, F. (1996), *The Web of Life*, Doubleday, NY

Code of Canon Law, (1999) (Can. 992-997) *Indulgences; Enchiridion Indulgentiarum, 4th ed.*, (online) http://en.wikipedia.org/wiki/Indulgence#History_of_indulgences (Accessed 20 December 2010)

Dolley, T. (2010), "Reclaiming our Animal Body", p. 82, in McCain, M. (Ed.), *GreenSpirit: Path to a New Consciousness*, O Books, Hants, UK

Eisler, R. (1988), *The Chalice and the Blade*, HarperCollins, San Francisco

Fox, M. (2000), *Original Blessing*, Tarcher/Putnam Ed edition

Fox, M. (2010), "Something is Amiss in the World of Religion", p.

82, in McCain, M. (Ed.), *GreenSpirit: Path to a New Consciousness*, O Books, Hants, UK

Gibbon, E. (1782, 1845), (Accessed 27 December 2010), The Project Gutenberg EBook of *The History of The Decline and Fall of the Roman Empire*, (Ed. David Widger) Release Date: June 7 2008 (EBook #25717), Last Updated: May 9, 2009 (Online), http://www.gutenberg.org/files/25717/25717-h/files/731/731-h/gib1-15.htm#2HCH0001

Gill, V. (2009), *The first glimpse of dark matter?* BBC News 18 December 2009, http://news.bbc.co.uk/1/hi/8420089.stm (Accessed 20 December 2010)

Hanh, T.N. (2003), *Creating True Peace*, Rider, Random House, London

Hansen, Ruedy, Sato and Lo (2010), *Global Surface Temperature Change*, http://data.giss.nasa.gov/gistemp/paper/gistemp2010_draft0601.pdf (Accessed 20 December 2010)

Hardin, J. (2004), *Gaia Eros*, Career Press, NJ

Harding, S. (2006), *Animate Earth*, Green Books, Dartington, UK

Ho, M. (2008), *The Rainbow and the Worm*, 3rd Edition, World Scientific Publishing Co., Singapore

Ho, M. and Popp, F. (1989) *Gaia and the Evolution of Coherence*, (Online) http://www.i-sis.org.uk/gaia.php (Accessed 15 February 2011)

Hyde, B. (2004), *Attending to the Felt Sense*, (Online) http://www.aare.edu.au/04pap/hyd04476.pdf, (Accessed 20 December 2010)

Hummel, C. (1986), *The Galileo Connection*, InterVarsity Press, pp. 27-29, in

Henderson, T., *Christian Answers Network*, (Online) http://www.christiananswers.net/q-eden/galileo.html (Accessed 20 December 2010)

Johnston, G., The Galileo Affair, Scepter Press, New Jersey, in

Henderson, T., *Christian Answers Network*, (Online) http://www.christiananswers.net/q-eden/galileo.html, (Accessed 20

December 2010)

Kessler, J.J., *Giordano Bruno: The Forgotten Philosopher*, (Online) http://www.infidels.org/library/historical/john_kessler/giordano_bruno.html (Accessed 20 December 2010)

King, A. (1996), *Spirituality: Transformation and Metamorphosis*, Religion 26:343–51, *From Earth and Nature-Based Spirituality (Part I): From Deep Ecology to Radical Environmentalism*, Bron Taylor, (Online) http://www.religionandnature.com/bron/arts/Taylor--Religion31(2).pdf (Accessed 20 December 2010)

King, U. (2009), *The Search for Spirituality*, Canterbury Press, Norwich

Kingsolver, B. (1988), *The Bean Trees*, Harper Collins, NY

Koestler, A. (1959), *The Sleepwalkers*, Penguin Books by arrangement with Hutchinson, London

Koestler, A. (1976), *The Ghost in the Machine*, Danube Edition, Hutchinson, London

Krishnamurti, J. (1969), *Krishnamurti Meditations* (Online) http://www.holybooks.com/krishnamurti-meditations-1969/ (Accessed 20 December 2010)

Lerner, Rabbi M. (2001), *What Is to What Ought to-Be, Enlightenment Next Magazine*, Spring/Summer, (Online) http://www.enlightennext.org/magazine/j19/lerner.asp?page=2 (Accessed 20 December 2010)

Lipton, B. (2005), *The Biology of Belief*, Cygnus Books, Llandeilo, UK

Lucille, F. (2009), *Eternity Now*, Non-Duality Press, Salisbury, UK

MacMullen, R. (1997), *Christianity and Paganism in the Fourth to Eighth Centuries*, Yale University Press, New Haven and London

McGilchrist, I. (2009), *The Master and His Emissary*, Yale University Press, New Haven and London

Mabry, J. (1994), *Cyberspace and the Dream of Teilhard de Chardin*, in Creation Spirituality Magazine, Summer 1994 text from (Online) http://theoblogical.org/dlature/united/ph2paper/noosph.html (Accessed 20 December 2010)

Margulis, L. (1999), *The Symbiotic Planet*, Orion Books, London

Merchant, C. (1982), *The Death of Nature*, Harper & Row, Wildwood House, London

Michell, J., *The Celtic Druids*, Britannia Internet Magazine (Online) http://www.britannia.com/wonder/michell2.html (Accessed 3 January 2011)

Popper, K.R. (1980), *The Logic of Scientific Discovery*, Routledge & Kegan Paul, London

Primavesi, A. (2000), *Sacred Gaia,* Routledge, London

Primavesi, A. (2003), *Gaia's Gift*, Routledge, London

Raymond, J. (2010), "On Christ", p. 148, in McCain, M. (Ed.), *GreenSpirit: Path to a New Consciousness*, O Books, Hants, UK

Rohr, J. (1988), (Ed.) *Science & Religion (Opposing Viewpoints)*, Greenhaven Press, p. 24, in Henderson, T., *Christian Answers Network* (Online) http://www.christiananswers.net/q-eden/galileo.html (Accessed 20 December 2010)

Sheldrake, R. (1981), *A New Science of Life: The Hypothesis of Formative Causation*, J. P. Tarcher, LA

Starhawk, (2001), *Religion From Nature, Not Archaeology*, in *Starhawk Responds to the Atlantic Monthly January 5, 2001* (Online) http://www.starhawk.org/pagan/religion-from-nature.html (Accessed 20 December 2010)

Szerszynski, B. (2005), *Nature, Technology and the Sacred*, Blackwell Publishing, Malden, MA, USA

Swimme, B. (1996), *The Hidden Heart of the Cosmos*, Orbis Books, N.Y.

Swimme, B. (2010), "What are Humans For", in McCain, M. (Ed.), *GreenSpirit: Path to a New Consciousness*, O Books, Hants, UK

Taylor, S. (2005), *The Fall*, O Books, Winchester, UK

Turnipseed,T. (2005), *Ecocide*, http://www.commondreams.org/views05/0722-30.htm (Accessed 29 November 2010)

White, L., Jr. (1967) "The Biological Roots of Our Ecological Crisis", in *Science* Vol 155, #3767, March 10, pp. 1203-07

Zeland, V. (2008), *Reality Transurfing 1: The Space of Variations*, O Books, Winchester, UK

BOOKS

O is a symbol of the world, of oneness and unity. In different cultures it also means the "eye," symbolizing knowledge and insight. We aim to publish books that are accessible, constructive and that challenge accepted opinion, both that of academia and the "moral majority."

Our books are available in all good English language bookstores worldwide. If you don't see the book on the shelves ask the bookstore to order it for you, quoting the ISBN number and title. Alternatively you can order online (all major online retail sites carry our titles) or contact the distributor in the relevant country, listed on the copyright page.

See our website **www.o-books.net** for a full list of over 500 titles, growing by 100 a year.

And tune in to myspiritradio.com for our book review radio show, hosted by June-Elleni Laine, where you can listen to the authors discussing their books.

mySpiritRadio